Aunt Mary
in the
Granary

and Other Prairie Stories

Eileen Comstock

FIFTH
HOUSE
PUBLISHERS

Front cover photograph painting by Hubert Theroux
Back cover photograph Carl Jr., Betty, and Kay
All photographs from the author's collection
Design by Articulate Eye

The publisher gratefully acknowledges the support of The Canada Council for the Arts and the Department of Canadian Heritage.

THE CANADA COUNCIL   LE CONSEIL DES ARTS
FOR THE ARTS   DU CANADA
SINCE 1957   DEPUIS 1957

We acknowledge the financial support of the Government of Canada through the Book Publishing Industry Development Program for our publishing activities.

Printed in Canada.

00 01 02 03 04/ 5 4 3 2

Canadian Cataloguing in Publication Data
Comstock, Eileen, 1926–
  Aunt Mary in the granary and other prairie stories
  ISBN 1-894004-54-X
  1. Comstock, Eileen, 1926– 2. Frontier and pioneer
life—Saskatchewan. 3. Kopperud family. I. Title.
FC3524.1.C65A3 2000   971.24'02   C00-910882-3
F1072.C65 2000

Fifth House Ltd.
A Fitzhenry & Whiteside Company
1511-1800 4 St. SW
Calgary, Alberta, Canada
T2S 2S5
1-800-387-9776

To the family I grew up in,
and to my children, who kept asking for
stories about "when I was little!"

❖

Table of Contents

Introduction

Agriculture in Saskatchewan had more than half a century of history before I was born in 1926. In the Qu'Appelle Valley, along the North and South Saskatchewan Rivers, in Wood Mountain, and a few other areas, people had broken sod, planted crops, and practised subsistence farming since about 1850. In the late 1800s ranchers herded cattle north to Canada and established sprawling ranches on the central plains where buffalo used to forage. The "Turkey Track" near Swift Current and, to the west and south, the "76" ranch ran immense herds. A horrific blizzard in 1906 killed thousands of cattle, and, at about the same time, homesteaders started to arrive in that part of Saskatchewan, so the days of large-scale ranching came to an end.

Surveyors measured and staked out the prairie, planting "monuments," legal survey marker posts, at the corner of every square mile. A homesteader could lay claim to a block one-half mile square (160 acres, or a quarter section) for ten dollars. If in the next three years he broke and cultivated thirty acres, built a home and a barn, and lived on the land six months out of each year, the land became his own. He was also allowed to buy a nearby quarter at three dollars an acre, called a "pre-emption," giving him a half-section farm, or 320 acres.

Our area, the Boule Creek district, about forty-five miles south of Swift Current, saw its first homesteaders about 1905. Homes varied. Some families had sold farms in densely settled areas of Minnesota or North Dakota and immigrated to a land where their growing sons could get farms of their own. They used some of the proceeds from their former home to build two-storey houses with three or four bedrooms. It may sound lush, but with large families—sometimes ten or eleven people living in each—the space was well used. Men who came on their own, with little backing, built shelters only big enough to contain a bed, a table, and a stove. The smaller it was, the easier to heat, and as long as it filled the homestead requirement it would do. Many of these shacks evolved into chicken coops, garages, or granaries as soon as a wife and children were accumulated and better housing acquired.

They were called "mixed" farms as they had chickens, pigs, and cattle for food and for sale, as well as horses to pull the machinery and provide transportation. By the late 1920s most farmers had a car or truck, and some had small gas tractors that powered threshing machines and grain choppers. Families grew most of their own food. With eggs to pick, chickens and pigs to feed, cows to milk, butter to churn, and big gardens to weed and harvest, there was no lack of meaningful work for all available hands, little and big.

Life was geared to the speed of animals, especially horses. Horses need rest at midday and were seldom worked after supper—not like today when giant tractors can keep going past the operator's point of exhaustion. There was often time to go to ball practice or visit the neighbours after the day's work. Families were close. Every day, children saw what their fathers and mothers did to make a living, and they could help. Even the five-year-old who gathered the eggs or helped weed the garden knew he was appreciated. It was a good time to be a child.

The stories in *Aunt Mary in the Granary and Other Prairie Stories* are true, to the best of my knowledge. My sister and I sometimes differ on details, such as just who was responsible for what, but if she wants to tell her side of it, she will just have to write her own book!

❖

Dad's old Case threshing machine

FARM AUCTIONS

*A local auction recalls
the time when
Dad "sold out"*

Robins and crows are back, and swans, geese, and ducks are squawking in the slough across the road. Treetops thicken against the sky as their leaf buds swell. Mother Nature isn't the only one heralding the coming of spring. The post office does its part by distributing dozens, or even hundreds, of auction-sale flyers in yellow, pink, red, green, and blue. Farm auctions are the true herald of the new season.

Farmers like going to auction sales. There is an empty time in spring that reminds me of the last week or two of pregnancy. Everything is ready to go, but it is not yet time. No use starting anything serious when you may never get the chance to finish it. Pregnant women bake cookies to put in the freezer. Farmers go to auction sales.

Getting ready for an auction is a tedious and nostalgic job. Current equipment must be cleaned up and cleaned out. Lost tools, long ago replaced, suddenly appear in little nooks and crannies—just in time to be passed on to someone else. Old, inefficient, or unreliable implements, kept for spare parts, have to be hauled out from fence corners. You never can tell what people will buy at an auction, sometimes paying more than the cost of a new item, so everything must be put up for bids: scrap iron, dying or dead motors, blacksmith tools not used since the days of horses, equipment hoary enough to be antiques, buggies, harnesses, rusty bolts in rusty tobacco cans, the cream separator, the welder. In short, the history of a farm and the farmer is laid out in the yard in long rows.

Serious bidders show up several hours early to inspect larger machinery and kick tires. Others gravitate to the hayracks and flat-bed trailers to look at the small stuff and investigate boxes full of odds and ends that will go for a dollar or two each. A guy might stumble across something he's been seeking for ages. About half the "buyers" come to visit with each other and see how the prices run, and there are a few honest souls who will admit they have come for the lunch. Lunch, provided by the local women's community club, usually includes homemade pie.

My dad farmed until he was seventy-five. He had certainly served his term and deserved to retire, but Ev and I and the rest of the family wondered how Dad would cope. So many men seemed to just wither and die once their farm was gone.

On sale day the sky was grey and overcast—just about the way I felt. The yard filled with strangers; even the neighbours seemed like strangers that day. We had been out to the farm the day before the sale. Dad told us kids to help ourselves to anything we wanted. I picked out a post drill that had been fastened to the car-shed wall all the days of my childhood, and I remembered how I used to turn the handle and pretend to drill holes when I was barely tall enough to reach it.

The sale went pretty well. Uncle Jul served as the clerk. Every once in a while Dad would come and sit with him, each brother trying to put on a cheerful face for the other. The old Case threshing machine, with which Dad had threshed his grain and many of his neighbours' crops for over thirty years, went to a buyer from south of Beaver Valley. The farmhouse was the last thing to go. The buyer made plans to move it off its foundation and out of the district. I watched the sale, and I watched my dad. I could hardly bear it.

That was thirty years ago. This spring one of our neighbours is selling out—the first from our generation, people we grew up with, whose kids went to school with ours. Our women's club is serving lunch, and, yes, there will be homemade pie. I hope there is a good crowd and that the day will be sunny and calm. But I can't say I'm looking forward to going.

Farm auctions are part of prairie life. I guess they're necessary—and a sort of recycling as one generation follows another. Farmers must retire but the land remains, still growing food for a hungry world. Younger feet will tread the hills and ravines and learn each acre by heart.

The old Case threshing machine still stands in the yard where Dad left it. Nobody ever came to get it, and I am kind of glad. As for Dad, well, he didn't wither away. On one of our visits, three or four years later, we found him practising his violin. He tucked the fiddle under his chin and looked up to the far corner of the room as his big fingers romped their way through "Turkey in the Straw," "The Devil's Dream," and "Beautiful Ohio." He explained that he had to practise because he'd been asked to go to the retirement home the next Sunday afternoon to play for the "old folks."

HOUSECLEANING

A woeful week
in spring and fall

When I was a kid, my childhood home was not fit to live in for a week or so each spring and fall. The timing depended on the weather. In fall, we'd start the job when the cold nights promised imminent winter storms. In spring, we'd wait for the snow to vanish, but we'd get cracking before Dad became too busy with fieldwork. It was called housecleaning. Nowadays we clean house more continuously, thanks to vacuums, dishwashers, and other handy appliances. Back then it was a twice-a-year ordeal for the entire family.

It all started with boxes. Our home, like most houses of the time, was small and short of closets and storage space, so a lot of stuff was put in boxes under the bed, or up in the attic. Dad hoisted himself up through the square hole in the ceiling and handed down boxes of summer dresses and sneakers in spring, and underwear, overshoes, sweaters, and jackets in fall. Mom checked to see what still fit us and packed last season's wear into the same boxes for Dad to lift back into the attic.

Then came chaos. Room by room, Mom washed windows, walls, and curtains, aired mattresses and bedding, beat rugs outside, and sometimes kalsomined walls and varnished woodwork. Then she scrubbed and waxed the floor. Dad helped with the ceilings and heavy lifting, and also washed windows outside and installed or removed the storm windows. Pictures, ornaments, and odds and ends Mom didn't know what to do with went onto the table in the kitchen for further consideration. Mom's back became sore, her hands raw, and her temper short. Meals were catch as catch can. We ate a lot of eggs.

The kitchen was the last and also the worst. All doors were shut to the rest of the house when the coal and wood stove was scraped clean, inside and out, and stove-pipes taken outside to have the soot banged and scratched out of them. No matter how carefully they're handled, stove-pipes are treacherous. Pipes can leak soot from either end, even when plugged with wadded newspaper. They come apart when they aren't supposed to and never go together without a struggle. It takes two people to manage the job, and they're usually not speaking to each other by the time it's done.

Then cupboards were excavated and scoured, and the seldom-used good dishes from the top shelf washed and returned to their place of honour. After being scrubbed, the walls, ceiling, and woodwork were given a fresh coat of oil paint, which took hours to dry. It was a couple of days before your eyes stopped watering. The next few days were devoted to the basement and to starching, ironing, and rehanging the curtains. That was almost a holiday compared to the start of the week.

We had been married five years before electricity came to the farm, so I put in a few years housecleaning the same way Mother had. Now, with better housing and modern equipment, we clean in bits and pieces and I don't miss the old way at all—except for one thing. I never have that wonderful feeling of accomplishing the near-impossible: having absolutely everything clean and tidy all at the same time.

Moving the brooder house to new ground was an annual spring chore.

THE FAKE HEN

*How my little sister
became mother
to twenty-four*

The closest connection most farm women have with chickens these days is either ready-to-cook chicken parts from the grocery store's freezer section, or else their feather pillows. It was not always so. Back in the very early days of farming on the Prairies, farmers allowed chickens to follow their natural instincts.

In springtime, after a short and noisy romantic encounter, the hens became "broody." A broody hen sought solitude. She abandoned the chicken coop and barnyard, found a cosy nook under a lilac bush, and scooped out a dusty hollow for her nest. There she laid an egg each day, until she had a collection of a dozen or so fertile eggs. For the next twenty-one days, she sat on them to keep them warm, leaving only for short intervals to get food and water.

Fertile eggs remain viable for several weeks after being laid. The embryos start to develop only when eggs are kept warm under the setting hen. Because the mother doesn't turn on the heat until all the eggs have been laid, all of them are ready to hatch at the same time. After the babies peck their way out of their shells, Mother Hen, whose temper has been decidedly bad during the three weeks on the nest, becomes a devoted nurse and mentor, teaching her fluffy, yellow children how to scratch for food and run for cover when a hawk or fox threatens. She also fiercely defends her family from any intruder, no matter how big. The chicks imprint on her—the first large, moving thing they see after hatching—and they follow her until their down turns into grown-up feathers.

Mechanization of chicken rearing arrived when small incubators became popular. Rather than rely on the hit and miss of an individual hen's initiative, Mom and Dad acquired a one-hundred-egg incubator. After enough fertile eggs had been collected to fill the incubator, the roosters were turned into canned chicken. For the rest of the year, the hens continued to lay, and any eggs that we didn't need at home were sold at the store or shipped to packers. The egg cheque was considered "Mother's money," although most of it went to buy groceries.

Once my parents had mastered the one-hundred-egg incubator, they decided that bigger was better. Dad bought a three-hundred-egg incubator at an auction sale. It was too large to get into the basement, so he set it up in a corner of the bedroom. The smaller incubator was heated by warm water from a pipe that ran above a kerosene lamp, but the bigger one used warm air heated by the lamp and was much more difficult to heat evenly. We had to sprinkle water on the eggs twice a day, when they were turned, as the warm air was too drying. And the thing stunk, something we hadn't noticed when it was in the basement.

At the half-time mark, when the eggs were candled— examined in front of a bright light to see the shadow of a growing chick—about a third of the eggs were not developing and had to be discarded. After the twenty-one days were up, only thirty-seven chicks hatched out. The small incubator had produced eighty-five to ninety chicks, and a broody hen usually ended up with as many chicks as she had eggs. Our success rate was sliding backwards very quickly.

Dad left the eggs in the incubator another day, for insurance, and then put the unhatched eggs into the big, galvanized washtub and set it on the stoneboat in the yard, ready to haul away. Several hours later, my sister

Carolie found that about two dozen more chicks had hatched out in the tub. Either the jostling or the hot sun had stimulated the little things enough to let them break out of their shells. She lifted them out of the tub and came to the house to proclaim her discovery. The chicks followed her.

You guessed it: she was the first large, moving thing they saw, and they imprinted on her. Even after Dad relocated them to the brooder house, Carolie was their mother-hen figure every time she came near. She didn't cuddle them under her wing, show them how to scratch for food, or alert them to danger, but until they started to grow adult feathers, they considered her their own dear mother.

THE GENERAL STORE

*Coal shovels, pepper, and kerosene—
you could find them all in
the general store, and hear
a few tall tales to boot*

I whip through the aisles in the Co-op, pushing a cart, more or less consulting my list. If I'm not in a hurry, the list will bear very little resemblance to the contents of the cart. But if I do hurry, and stick to my list, I can finish my shopping in minutes. After all, grocery shopping isn't a social occasion any more.

It used to be. In Cadillac, Saskatchewan, our community meccas were Buckwold's general store on Centre Street, its high, white false front suggesting a second storey that never was, and Bdinka's, a low-ceilinged, dimmer place with shoe repair machines tucked in the back. These places hummed with shopping and chatting, especially on Saturdays.

On either side of the recessed front door, big, plate-glass windows that were supposed to entice passers-by with their attractive merchandise were usually filled with dusty, sun-faded reminders of somebody's short-lived enthusiasm for window displays, last year or maybe the year before. It really didn't matter, because the windows were so plastered with auction and meeting posters that no one could see the displays anyway.

The walls were lined with shelves almost to the ceiling.

Top shelves held miscellaneous items in low demand: galvanized pails, lanterns, bridles, lamp chimneys, or copper boilers. They were accessed by a ladder on wheels or, more riskily, by a long rod with a hook or clamp on the end. Lower shelves held cans, cereal boxes, spices, baking powder, soap flakes, vanilla, bolts of cloth, tobacco tins—a great assortment. The storekeeper and clerks reigned in the aisle between the shelves and the counters that ringed the central area. The centre of the store was for customers.

Toward the back, a huge, potbellied coal heater sprouted stove-pipes that reached through the galvanized pressed-tin ceiling. A couple of captain's chairs and an assortment of apple boxes surrounded the heater for the convenience of the old gentlemen who met at the store every day for a gossip and a smoke—or a chew. Spitting on the oiled floor was not considered polite, so the chewers would saunter to the heater every once in a while, open the fire door, and expertly deposit their excess saliva onto the embers.

We kids spent a lot of time looking at the glass-fronted candy counter, deciding how to spend our Saturday nickel. Chocolate bars—Sweet Marie, O Henry, and Cadbury Milk Chocolate—were our favourites, but they cost a whole nickel each, so we were torn between them and the penny candy: little pink and yellow hearts with "I love you" or "Be mine" printed on them in red, five for a penny, or liquorice pipes and cigars with red beads indicating the lit end, and liquorice plugs that looked like real chewing tobacco, complete with a prong-backed tin label that could be fastened to a shirt collar—these were one cent each and lasted a long time. Big suckers on wooden sticks, peppermint canes, ribbon candy—oh, the penny candy in the big, square glass jars with silver lids took a lot of decision time.

Other neat equipment stood on the counter, too. A two-foot wheel of cheddar cheese sat under a glass cover on a whirligig contraption. It was cut into wedges by an axe-like knife hinged to a rod that stuck up out of the centre.

The clerk weighed the wedge on a white scale with pounds and ounces indicated by a pointer in the top, visible from both sides. Several rolls of brown paper in different widths unrolled from a holder at one end of the counter, right beside the string that reeled off a cone. Coffee beans were turned into little bits in the bright red coffee grinder, its hopper and base decorated with metal scrollwork flowers and vines, when the clerk turned the handle attached to a big flywheel.

The aroma of freshly ground coffee, the sharp odour of cheddar, a faint dusty, musty smell from the oiled floor, and the woody scent from newly unrolled brown paper gave the general store an ambience all its own.

No scanners or automatic tills then. As Mom read from her list, the clerk would move each item from its shelf to the countertop and write it down on the bill book. Each family had its own bill book. When everything was gathered, he added it up, with pencil on paper, and marked it paid or charged. If real money was involved, the till came into action. Keys on long levers activated little cards that popped up into the viewing glass so that the customer could make sure the correct keys were being pressed. The keys jangled, and the cash drawer opened and closed with metallic clunks.

When the ritual was over, the cans, paper bags, and string-tied parcels were packed into a cardboard wholesaler's carton retrieved from a back room. Mr. Buckwold usually tucked a wee paper bag of hard candy in among the groceries—a treat for the kids and often the only luxury item in the whole box.

When the groceries were unpacked, the sheets of brown paper and paper bags were smoothed out and folded, the string untied and added to the rolled-up ball in the "knives and forks" drawer, and the cartons saved for storing winter clothing in summer or the other way round, or for the mending, or for taking lunch to the field, or even for making paper-people houses. Recycling is not a recent invention.

I am not a child of the Thirties for nothing. I still come

home from shopping and fold paper grocery bags and smooth out sheets of brown paper. Boxes filled with empty boxes inhabit my workroom. I fully intend to take back to the store the plastic bags full of plastic bags I have tucked away. And I still wince when I find myself actually forced to buy string. There really should be a ball of it somewhere in the knives and forks drawer.

BUT DON'T GO NEAR THE WATER

The joy of swimming in Uncle Oliver's slough

"Mother, may I go swimming?"
"Yes, my darling daughter.
Hang your clothes on a hickory limb.
But don't go near the water."

—*Old nursery rhyme*

My sister and I lived for two special times each year. One, of course, was Christmas, and the other was our annual trip to Lac Pelletier, where we did our best to become waterlogged every day. Memories of the lake popped up all year long, especially in spring, when our two-mile walk to school took us past several sloughs. Whether the breeze wafted ripples to lap on the shore, or a brisk wind made real waves, or a dead calm made fleecy clouds reflect on the shallow water, one of us would be sure to say to the other, "Doesn't that remind you of the lake?" And it always did.

One Saturday, early in May, we went looking for crocuses in Uncle Oliver's pasture, across the road from home. The sun was hot; new grass showed green through last year's dead thatch; red-winged blackbirds perched on

❖

Carolie and Eileen Kopperud, c. 1930

stalks of last year's cattails, loudly proclaiming their territory. Down in the little valley, the slough winked and beckoned to us as the sun glinted on its surface. It was just too much to resist.

First, we took off our socks and running shoes and gingerly tiptoed through the prickly stalks of dead grass at the edge. The water was warm—in fact, it was just fantastic. It became blissfully cool as we waded knee-deep, and we could just feel the sticky sweat rolling off us. We held up our skirts and ventured farther. A sudden hole took me by surprise—not a big hole, just deep enough to soak the bottom of my underwear. We decided that we really should have taken off more clothing because it would be a shame to get our dresses wet "accidentally."

It took about three minutes to scramble back to shore, strip completely, and get back into the water. The water never did get any deeper than mid-thigh, except for the odd depression that horses' hooves had made when the slough was nearly dry the previous year, but by scrunching up and half-kneeling, we found it easy to pretend that we were in deep water, water deep enough to swim in, if we could swim. We did a lot of splashing and yelling, and occasionally overbalanced enough to thoroughly wet our heads. It was wonderful.

I don't know how long we "swam," but eventually our consciences took hold and we realized that if we didn't go home soon, Mom would worry. Drying off was a problem, as was getting our feet clean enough to reinsert them into socks and shoes. There was a tacit agreement that we wouldn't tell anybody that we'd gone into the slough—not that it had been forbidden, but silence was often safer than blabbing everything we knew.

When we were once again covered and decent, we hurriedly plucked a few crocuses and walked home. It was nearly dinnertime. Mother accepted the crocuses, arranged them on a saucer because the stems were so short, and gave us several sharp looks. "Were you girls in the water?" she inquired.

I don't know what gives parents the instinct to ask

questions like that, right out of the blue. Even after I was a parent myself, I would surprise myself by asking similar questions out of the blue, not always impelled by evidence, but by a naturally suspicious mind that seems to come spontaneously with parenthood. What that does is to reinforce, in a child's mind, belief in the supernatural, which is not always a bad thing.

"Were you girls in the water?" The question hung in the air for a breath or two while we mentally reviewed our options. We weren't above fudging the truth a smidge—little white lies, very little ones, were sometimes overlooked—but a straight "no" would have been an out-and-out lie. So we told the truth and reported everything about our marvellous swim. In fact, we tried by our enthusiasm to evoke in our mother a deep longing to go for a swim in Uncle Oliver's slough. It did not work.

Mother gave us a lecture about the danger of going into the water without a grownup nearby, and told us that it was entirely too early in the year to go swimming because we might get chilled and catch a cold. We did manage to extract the concession that June weather would probably be warm enough for swimming.

By the first of June, Uncle Oliver's slough had nearly dried up. The only slough with water was down in our own pasture. It wasn't even up to our knees and was slightly green and just a bit smelly. We went in anyway. We had to lie down and roll around just to get wet all over, and it wasn't much fun.

We also got the itch. For three days, we scratched and fussed and reminded our mother hourly that she had said it was all right to swim in June.

I haven't swum in a slough since then. The memory of the itch is just as vivid as the memory of our wonderful May swim. However, whenever I walk past an expanse of shallow water, shining and rippling in the sun, it does remind me of the lake.

BLUE MILK AND CREAM

*Going to
the produce shelf
beats going for the cows*

Milk occupies about twenty feet of the dairy wall in our local Co-op. Skim, 2%, whole, half and half, chocolate, cartons, jugs, sour cream, cottage cheese, yogurt—oh, the variety is endless. And no work or mess involved nowadays. Just money. But a few decades ago, it was a different story. Milk production used to be a major part of a farmer's work, and the chores involved even dribbled down to the kids.

Our attitude toward cows depended on the circumstance. We enjoyed "going for the cows," a leisurely trip on foot or bareback to the pasture, where a kid could imagine herself an explorer, a pioneer, or a heroine of the Old West, perhaps snare a gopher or two, look for arrowheads (not that we ever found any), or gather crocuses and buffalo beans to present to Mom.

Much as we liked working with Dad, we were not keen on helping pitch loose hay onto the high rack or tramping stacks under a scalding sun. Pumping the water trough full or filling the chop boxes and hay mangers wasn't bad, but cleaning the barn left a lot to be desired as a pastime, especially as Dad was pretty particular about the result.

Pail feeding newly weaned week-old calves was fun. Their instinct was to nurse with their heads up, so we had to let them suck our fingers and then lower hand and all into the milk pail. They snuffled and sneezed but soon caught on. It wasn't as much fun when they grew big enough to bunt us about in their eagerness to get at the warm milk.

We girls didn't often have to help with milking, except during seeding or harvest—which, coincidentally, was when the flies were bad. Cows have efficient fly swatters, and there is nothing quite like a swat on the face, bare neck, or arms by the wiry tuft of a dry tail or, worse yet, a muddy tail to lessen enthusiasm for milking.

Setting up the cream separator and operating it was a regular chore for kids. We cranked and cranked. As the separator picked up speed, the ding of the bell turned into a click that indicated it was time to turn the tap to let the milk flow. Centrifugal force separated the lighter cream from the skimmed milk. After the cream and milk were separated, the work wasn't over. Every morning we had to dismantle the darned thing and wash the pieces. We couldn't use soap in the first wash because the milk residue made the dishcloth, your hands, and everything else slimy, so there had to be two washes, then a warm rinse and a scalding rinse. About twenty discs had to be reassembled in the original sequence. It was a messy business.

We seldom use cream now, and we drink 2% milk. Back then, we drank skim milk—our town cousins called it blue milk—but filling the cream jug was always part of setting the table. We put cream on everything from porridge and pudding to our favourite snack: a slice of white bread soaked in cream and covered with brown sugar. Nobody worried about calories (perhaps they hadn't been invented yet).

Butter was made in a wooden churn. Sour cream had to be the right temperature or else it would turn into a foamy mess and the butter wouldn't come, prompting Mom to pour hot water from the tea kettle into the churn. We drank the fresh buttermilk and gave the excess to the pigs. Freshly churned butter was squished around in cold-water baths until all the buttermilk had been washed out. Then it was salted and packed into crocks, or moulded into pound blocks and wrapped in parchment paper to be sold in town. When we had too much cream, we sent it by train to the Moose Jaw dairy in squat, shiny cream cans. The cream cheque helped to pay the grocery bills.

Those days are fun to relive in memory, but I am happy to leave them there. Sure, we used to get our milk for free, but take my word for it—it is easier and considerably neater to find the money to buy it.

AUNT MARY IN THE GRANARY

In which the terrorized become terrors

My sister and I had walked a mile or more across the fields for an overnight visit with a school friend several years older than we were. Sarah's mother had grown up in Ireland and that same day was entertaining another family and their grandfather, who had also grown up on the Green Isle. We girls didn't do much playing that day. It was far more interesting to sit quietly and listen to stories about banshees, foretellings, and other eerie Irish folktales. The two expatriates seemed to believe each other, and no sooner was one story finished than an even spookier tale would begin. We were particularly intrigued by the superstition of the "death knock," which was three knocks high on a wall. That was the way a death in Sarah's mother's family was "foretold."

After supper we girls were sent a half-mile to fetch some milk. As we walked back under the moonlit sky, Sarah confided that they had just hauled her Aunt Mary from the train station. Aunt Mary was from Ireland, and she needed to be buried.

Apparently, there was a terrific shortage of cemetery land in Ireland. After a person had been buried for twelve years, she was expected to have returned to dust and ashes, and her plot was reused. Aunt Mary, however, had been embalmed and was nearly as good as new when dug up. Rules were rules, though, so she had to be shipped to her nearest relative in Canada, where there was lots of room to bury people.

Carolie and I were sceptical. We were passing some granaries about then, and Sarah said, "Well, come here and I will prove it." She set down the milk pail, took our hands, led us into the open granary, and plunked our hands down onto something cold, damp, and meaty, lying on a trestle just inside the door. Sceptical or not, the day's fund of stories had made its mark on us. We panicked, and even when our friend tried to tell us it was just the carcass of a pig that had been butchered earlier that day, we were determined to go home, right now, across the fields, in the dark.

Sarah knew she would be in trouble if we did, so she finally talked us around. The main inducement to stay was the idea that we should knock three times on the wall and see if her mother thought it was a "foretelling."

We walked around the house and, peeking through the window, saw her mother sitting in a rocking chair. Sarah found a hoe, and while we watched, she tapped three times, high on the wall behind her mother.

All hell broke loose. The poor woman sprang from her chair, ran to the door, and started screaming for her husband and her daughter. I guess the day's storytelling had worked on her imagination, too. Her husband came from the barn, carrying the lantern, and we three sauntered up to the door, trying to look innocent.

It took quite a while for her to calm down, and I am sorry to say that none of us had the sense or the nerve to tell her what the three knocks really were. We took our shame and guilt to bed with us.

Long after the other two were asleep, I opened my eyes and saw a faint light wavering across the ceiling. I *knew* it was just the reflection of the lantern carried by Sarah's father as he went to check on the animals for the last time that night. But then on the other hand, maybe—it could—just perhaps—be a banshee!

OLD WIVES' TALES

Tall tales
that we believed—
for the most part

I once knew a lot of things that weren't true. I actually *knew* them then. I'm not too sure where I acquired all this knowledge, because everybody else my age knew the same things, so it couldn't have been just from my grandmother, although she did pass on a few choice bits.

For instance we *knew* that if you ate raw chokecherries and drank milk, you'd be poisoned. We four cousins ate an awful lot of raw chokecherries when the relatives all went to the War Holes to pick berries—but you can bet that none of us drank any milk for the rest of the day. And we never got poisoned, which proves something or other.

We knew that if you cut a snake in two, it wouldn't stop wiggling until sundown. Dad had ploughed out a bunch of sods in a slough near home, from which he made a sod henhouse. We made playhouses from the leftovers, and the garter snakes flocked into them to keep cool, so we cut quite a few in half to experiment. We were never allowed to stay there till sundown, so we couldn't be sure they all quit wiggling at the same time, but we *knew* they would. And we were pretty sure the ones that just lay still had a few wiggles in them, because the sun wasn't down yet.

We also knew that if you killed a rattlesnake, its mate would follow you forever, bent on revenge. We made quite sure none of the snakes we killed had rattles on, just in case, but we kind of doubted this "follow you forever" bit anyhow. Suppose you got in an airplane and went to live in China? How would the rattlesnake get across the ocean?

We knew that the cows and horses in the barn all knelt down at midnight on Christmas Eve and could talk for a few minutes. We were always asleep long before that, so we never heard them. They probably spoke in Norwegian, anyway, because the language used in church was Norwegian. I was always going to find out which language they spoke when I got older, but I never have.

We knew there were two kinds of diabetes: sugar diabetes and water diabetes. If you had sugar diabetes and ate any sugar at *all*, you'd die. Same with drinking water, if you had the other kind. We thought we would rather have water diabetes because one could live a pretty good life on pop and milk and coffee. Had to be careful brushing teeth, though.

We knew that bulls became vicious at the sight of red. Mr. Haakenson had a bull in the corral, and when we took a shortcut to school through his land, we hid our red lard-pail lunchkits under our jackets and stuffed any red mittens into our pockets. The most timid of us even clamped lips together so no red showed, but I figured if the bull could see that well, our red cheeks would be the end of us anyway.

Grandma told us that if girls whistled in the house, the devil danced, and if we told lies, dragonflies would sew our lips together with their tails. She had a twinkle in her eye, but we wouldn't have believed the dragonfly one anyway. There were always dragonflies around, and we knew our lips had never been fastened shut, not that we were great liars, but we usually had one or two on our conscience. If she were trying to curb our whistling—tough. We thought it would be neat to make the devil dance.

Occasionally Dad bought the *Toronto Star Weekly*. The main attraction was five double pages of "funnies." The magazine section usually featured several sensational horror stories, gorily illustrated, involving Oriental opium rings, torture, and general underworld menaces. I read

Mom and Eileen, ready to go berry picking at the Wise Creek coulee

everything, whether I understood it or not. Mother always cautioned my sister and me never to take a ride from anyone we didn't know well because we might be sold into "white slavery." We walked two miles to school and I seldom remember getting the chance to get a ride anyway, but we were careful. I knew just what would happen: we'd be sold, put into cages, and sent down South, where we would have to pick cotton for the rest of our lives.

We didn't fall for just anything. We knew some stories were simply fairy tales. We didn't come right out and say that we didn't believe them. After all, if we admitted knowing about the tooth fairy, we'd probably end up not getting money under the pillow. Santa, of course, was one of the uncles, but we were always too excited at the time to figure out which one was missing. A baby from a cabbage patch, or brought by the stork, was just silly to a farm kid. We thought it probably was just the grownups' way of talking politely about something they found embarrassing. Besides, there were dozens of babies around, and we had never seen a stork anywhere in Saskatchewan. The Sandman, well, maybe; he was supposed to be invisible and our eyes sure did get scratchy.

Now that I'm getting to be a bit of an "old wife" myself, I know that some odd things really are true. If I hear of something twice, it will pop up a third time, whether it is an unusual fact or something in the news, or even an unexpected death. Also, if I'm in a rotten mood, people around me will be thoughtless, annoying, and generally nasty all day. If I buy something rather extravagant, the next two stores I enter will have the same thing on sale. When my hair is a mess and I'm wearing my shabbiest clothes to paint the ceiling or clean the stove, people will drop in all day. Of course I can't say that these things are "old wives' tales." They are plain truth—ask anyone.

OH, YOU MEAN
THE TOALET!

A little
house on the prairie

When I was growing up, every home, every church, every school had a little building or two out back. They came in all colours or none, all sizes, and all kinds of repair. Some were discreetly screened with bushes or trees. Some just sat there boldly and serenely indispensable. There was a priggish disinclination to call a spade a spade in those days (although now a spade is usually called a backhoe). Many phrases were used to avoid saying "toilet." Common terms in our school were Mrs. Jones, house of parliament, back house, wee house, convenience, and even (I blush to admit) toy-toy. The big boys sometimes called it by its real name, sometimes by names even worse! We would love to have told the teacher on them but we either couldn't bring ourselves to repeat the words or were afraid the boys would find out who tattled.

During school hours we had to put up our hands and ask to "leave the room." If the teacher was busy or grumpy, she sometimes ignored the wildly waving hand and someone, usually in Grade One, would have an "accident." Children, being only semi-civilized, teased the victim at recess until tears flowed. One of our young lady teachers, seeking to avoid being interrupted in class, made the rule that if you wanted to sharpen your pencil, you should hold your pencil in the air, and if you had to "go," you should hold up two fingers. She would nod her head for permission and go on with her class. The pencil part was fine, but *two* fingers! We all knew what "number two" meant, and it was terribly embarrassing. Of course, we were easily embarrassed. To our youthful ears, "toilet water" was shocking. We had no idea it meant cologne.

In 1912 Grandpa Kopperud and his two eldest sons arrived in Saskatchewan early in spring. They dug a basement, built a barn, hired someone to build a house, broke some land, and managed other essentials just fine with a pole set across two posts over a hole in the ground. Several months later, Grandma and the six younger children arrived by train and were brought to their new home. Grandma approved of the house and the barn, but she was not impressed with the pole, the posts, or the hole in the ground. Dad said they had to start building the toilet that very evening.

Grandpa's toilet was well built, windproof, and had a small window way up high. The seat was low and, three-bear style, had a big hole, a middle-sized hole, and a wee hole with a built-in stool in front of it. It is still in service. It was always painted, inside and out. When my cousin and her husband took over the farm, she painted a staff and musical notes on the floor. I have no idea what the tune is, and my cousin isn't saying.

The nicest toilet in the neighbourhood had been insulated with layers of newspaper pasted on the walls and then wallpapered. There was linoleum on the floor. A little vase with crepe-paper flowers sat in the curtained window.

The most impressive feature of that outhouse was "boughten" toilet paper. Most of us made do with old catalogues, except at canning time, when we had the tissue paper from around peaches or pears, or at Christmas, from around Japanese oranges. One of our hired men was a fan of dime novels, and when he left, Mother found quite a stack of them. She didn't think they were proper reading for us, but her thrifty soul wouldn't let her burn up useful paper. So she put them in our toilet, where, of course, I read them all, even the ones where the end of the story had already been torn off. I spent a lot of time in the little house that year.

Some years ago, I toured Scandinavia and Britain with my two sisters and our daughters. We were shopping in downtown Lillehammer and couldn't see any sign pointing to a public washroom. We stopped an older Norwegian couple. "Could you tell me where there is a restroom?" I asked. They looked at one another and knit their brows. I rephrased the question, sure they spoke English, because nearly every Scandinavian does: "Could you tell me where is the ladies' bathroom?" I don't know if the girls just looked uncomfortable or what, but suddenly the man caught on. He said, in a *very* loud voice, "Oh, YOU MEAN THE TOALET," and pointed up the street. This taught us not to mince around. In Norway, you rest in a restroom and bathe in a bathroom, and when you want a toilet, you ask for the "toalet."

Travel broadens one's knowledge in unusual ways. I know now that flushing mechanisms vary greatly overseas. The handle can be on the top left of the tank, as in Canada, or in any of the other three corners. There may be, instead, a plunger to pull or push on the top of the tank. It may be a button or handle on the back wall, or a step-on button or lever on the floor. Once I checked all over and had nearly given up when I noticed a bell-pull rope hanging from the ceiling. I pulled it. That's what it was, all right. Another stumbling block, literally, was the bathroom door-sill in our Norwegian bed-and-breakfast. It was three inches high. I never seemed able to remember, and bifocals are no help either, so I lurched out into the corridor several times a day.

In Norway, they may have doorsills, but in Britain, they have something they pretend is toilet paper. It's the right shape and size, but the texture is peculiar—a lot like waxed paper, or else parchment paper for covering jelly jars. I always wondered about those poor imprisoned souls who used to fill their empty hours writing famous memoirs or great novels on toilet paper. I now believe it. Ink wouldn't run or smudge, nor could a pencil break through that sturdy stuff. We took samples home for souvenirs. The British government must have bought bales and warehouses of it, because when we returned six years later, public restrooms still had the same stuff, except maybe a bit stiffer than before.

Oh, we're all up to date now, and the wee house is no more. In her living-room, my daughter has planted a Swedish ivy in a china chamber pot. It's attractive and a good conversation starter. My grandmother would think it vulgar; my mother would applaud her ingenuity and thrift. Me, well, I'm just glad those days are over. Although, on a nice summer's day, with the door propped open, the birds scolding each other in the trees, and a lot of great reading material, I guess I could work up some nostalgia for the little house out back.

FERRY CROSSINGS

A prairie chicken
takes to
the ocean

One July when we were kids, our folks packed our old tent, firewood, blankets, the old couch, clothing, food, and all of us into and onto the Model T, and we set off for a week of camping at Clearwater Lake.

Dad shifted into low gear at the top of the two-mile slope down to Saskatchewan Landing, north of Swift Current. When we reached the valley floor, Carolie and I gazed awestruck at the most water we had ever seen in our lives. It looked a bit scary to us prairie chickens. We waited for the ferry, a large raft tethered to a cable, to come from the far side. The ferryman adjusted the angle at which it met the current so it was propelled across the stream by the flow of the South Saskatchewan River. Dad drove down the wooden ramp onto the ferry and we all got out of the car. Mom and Dad kept Carl and Kay within arm's reach, but Carolie and I were allowed to walk around on the deck—with warnings not to go near the edge.

We sang. We spent a lot of time singing back then, and the "Ferry Boat Serenade" seemed appropriate for our river crossing. I didn't approach the edge of the ferry but managed to be close enough to a big beam that, when the ferryman adjusted his cable, shifted and came down on the very toe of my running shoe. I was trapped. Luckily my toes weren't squashed, but I couldn't move. At age fourteen, I was far too embarrassed to let anybody know my predicament, so I just stood there singing until we got to the far side, when the beam shifted enough to release me.

Forty-some years later, ferries popped back into my life. When one of our steers was killed in our pasture, we found that our insurance policy did not cover death caused by humans or animals. On the other hand, if we herded our cattle onto a ferry to cross a river and any fell off and drowned, that was covered! We felt we could do without that clause here on the prairie.

When I arranged for our first trip overseas, the travel agent explained that there were only reclining seats available for the ferry trip from Newcastle, England, to Bergen, Norway, across the North Sea. Sounded fine to me—here on dry ground. Well, the ferry arrived in Newcastle four hours late, thanks to a storm at sea. Although the high winds had subsided by the time we boarded, the North Sea sulks after a storm, so the waves remained high all night. We each took Gravol to ward off seasickness, but we still had trouble walking across the rolling deck. It kept coming up to meet our feet, and just when we'd adjusted to walking uphill, the ferry went over the hump of the wave and tipped down the other side, turning the deck into a downhill slant.

After our long day of travelling to the ferry, we—my sisters Carolie and Kay and our three daughters—were ready to "recline" for the night. Kay and the girls took their wee, ferry-issue blankets and bedded down on the floor. Carolie and I tried it, but in spite of being well padded, our older bones couldn't adapt, so we went back to the seats. Even at the furthest "recline," we were still rather upright. Every time I dozed, my head started to fall off.

The next morning, after exploring the duty-free store and looking in vain for whales, we gathered on deck to see the skerries and the first glimpses of Norway, land of our forefathers. I found a sheltered nook and was feeling very sentimental about the whole thing. Unfortunately, my nook was right in front of the airhorn, and when it blew I thought the world had come to an end. It certainly cured any tender reflections.

We'd learned our lesson about reclining seats, so for our next few trips on North Sea ferries, we booked couchettes: bunk beds in small cubicles—way, way, way down at the bottom of the ship. Clean, comfortable, and cheap. Aha, I thought, that is the way to spend a night at sea. Until our last trip, from Hamburg, Germany, to Harwich, England. Apparently we had picked the same weekend that three or four hundred German teenagers were on a school-break tour to England. They kept losing one another and ran around, hollered, and slammed doors all night long. I am a bit deaf and can also sleep with a pillow over my head, but they broke through all my defences. And then I started hearing water noises from the bottom of the ship. It sounded as if I were only about three feet from lots and lots of saltwater. I came close to thinking fondly about reclining seats.

Anyhow, if we ever go again, I think I will mortgage anything I own, even my nearest and dearest, to get the extra $150 for a private cabin way up high on the top deck of the ferry. A prairie chicken can't stand to be too close to that much water.

*Mom and Dad (Carl and Elna Kopperud), packed for
camping at Lac Pelletier, Saskatchewan, c. 1941.
Note the ever-present coffee cup.*

THE MODEL T

Our magic chariot—
but only in summer

Dad took her down to the dugout for a bath on Saturday
mornings. He dried her until she was black and shiny, and
polished her windows inside and out. We didn't call her
Betsy or Lizzy or any cutie-pie name, although she was definitely female. In fact, we seldom used her family name,
"Ford." She went by her first name, "Model T."

By the time I remember her, she was rather mature, as
Dad had bought her in the early 1920s. Informal trips were
usually taken with horses. The Model T was reserved for
dress-up occasions, such as church, visits to Mom's sisters
in Vanguard or Rush Lake, the twice-yearly trips to Swift
Current, forty miles away, our summer camping at Lac
Pelletier, and Saturday-night shopping in Cadillac.

The Model T was boxy and plain, but in my child's eye
she had quite a human countenance. Her headlights were
widely spaced, prominent eyes, the hood that lifted up on
both sides of the engine formed a pair of shrugging shoulders, and on both sides of the wee mouth where the crank
was inserted like a crooked tongue, the radiator support
looked like a thin moustache. (Several women of our
acquaintance had moustaches, visible enough to soothe
any doubts about our Model T's gender.) The inside uphol-
stery was faded and wrinkly, as smooth and warm as
Grandma's cheek. As well as these human touches, she had

other attractive features. The windows were square and big enough to see the world without scrunching around, and they rolled all the way down so we kids could exit and enter without disturbing Mom in the front seat. There was a cryptic message on a little switch where the key went in. I know now that it referred to the battery, magneto, and lights. But then, Carolie and I thought the switch was named "Mag" and the message a flippant instruction on how to turn the lights off. It read: "Bat Dim Off On Mag."

The Model T was a man's car. It took a good deal of strength to start with the crank, to steer, and to pull back the lever to change gears. Finesse was needed to avoid breaking off the cranker's thumb if she backfired, and to know just when to flip the lever behind the steering wheel to take off the choke after the motor caught. Every once in a while, Dad would overhaul the engine. He laid a binder canvas out on the ground, and as he dismantled the motor, the parts were cleaned and laid out in progression on the canvas so they could be put back in reverse order. He had a neat little stick with a suction cup on the end that was used to rotate the valves in emery paste to reseat them. We girls coveted that suction cup—we could make it stick on our foreheads or palms—but we were prohibited from even approaching the canvas when Dad was operating.

As the year grew cold and chilly, Dad put an ash pan of hot embers on the dirt floor of the garage under the motor, and refilled the radiator with kettlefuls of hot water to warm the Model T so he could turn the crank. She had no heater, so we kids in the back seat and Mom in the front were swaddled in quilts to protect us from icy air just a floorboard away. Dad, even in wool socks and felt boots, often ended a trip with frostbitten toes. After snowfall, Dad jacked her up and set blocks under the axles to relieve the strain on the tires throughout her winter holiday.

She was a versatile old girl. Every July during summer holidays she became a combination van and travel trailer. Dad replaced her back seat with wooden egg crates full of food and dishes, padded the crates with pillows and bedding, laid the couch mattresses on the roof, and flipped a pull-out couch upside down on top of them. He fastened the couch down with ropes, wired the folded-up canvas tent and some firewood onto a running board, and drove us off to Lac Pelletier.

It was a two-hour trip and, for Carolie and me, the highlight of the year. One summer, so that we wouldn't have to miss a few minutes in the lake while Dad pitched the tent, we donned our woollen bathing suits under our slacks and blouses. The roads were poor and the day was hot. The trip lasted forever, and our homemade swimsuits became good and itchy. The only thing that took my mind off the itch was a trail along a sidehill on the east side of the lake. I knew in my heart that we would soon topple sideways and roll end over end into the lake. But the Model T always got us there and back safely. One year, when we were leaving, a heavy rain turned the steep, curvy road out of the valley into two rut rivers, but our vehicle made it to the top. About halfway home, we ran into a severe lightning storm. Dad realized that the legs of the metal couch sticking up from the roof had turned us into a travelling lightning rod, so we stopped at a farm along the highway until the storm was over.

Besides the crank start and lack of heat, there were a couple of other problems with our car. She had magnificent clearance, and the narrow wheels handled the deep-rutted trails easily. On a muddy road, she could split the difference and ride one edge and the ridge between. But there was a problem. When rain pounded on the windshield, the wiper had to be swished back and forth by hand, but because both hands were already busy as can be with "Armstrong steering" most of the time, the wiper wasn't often used. Then, as the car aged, the bands that put her into the forward gears grew worn and would slip on a hard uphill pull. I remember several times when she refused to advance more than halfway up the hill at Swift Current. Mom, Grandma, and we kids had to get out and walk up while Dad backed down, turned the car around, and chugged up in reverse, using those bands that were less worn.

In 1940, when crops were better and finances improved, Dad bought a '34 Chev. We were impressed by the fancy fenders, stick shift, and, best of all, four doors. No more crawling out the back window. The Model T sat in the yard for a couple of years until Orville Olson, a neighbour lad who worked for us one fall, bought it as his first car. I don't know where she went from there. My brother Carl and I sometimes wonder if she's maybe sitting in a shed somewhere, waiting for us to rescue her and bring her back into her family.

THE NIGHT OF
THE RODEO DANCE

*My sister and I pout,
and Mother defends
her territory*

Carolie and I pouted. We tried to tell our mother that at ten and twelve we sure were old enough to go to the pavilion for the dance! After all, we had been going to dances all our lives. (It seemed irrelevant that we'd gone to schoolhouse dances, where Dad played the violin, everybody in the district attended, and sleepy children could flake out on the desks in the corner.) But Mother stayed stubborn, and finally clamped her lips together, a sign that it would not be wise to continue the argument.

Dad had brought us to our yearly camp at Lac Pelletier, pitched our shabby tent, dug a hole behind the corner of the tent to hold sealers of milk and butter, poured in a couple of pails of water, and covered it with boards and gunny sacks. He had to return home for a few days to attend to chores, but would come back to the lake on Saturday. He waved good-bye to Carolie and me, as we were already in the lake, where we usually spent the entire day, and left Mother to cope with our toddler brother, baby sister, and us for three days.

On Friday, the usually quiet campground started to fill up with people coming to the 1938 two-day rodeo. A pair of real cowboys and their ladies set up a little square tent right next to us. It was so exciting, and one of the ladies

❖

The campsite at Lac Pelletier, complete with tent and Model T.
(L to R) Carl Jr., Carolie, Kay, and Eileen, 1938

was so beautiful. She had long, very bright blond hair, and wore lipstick and rouge and earrings, even in the daytime! And she had cowboy boots and a fringed skirt and a western shirt and a string tie! And she was really nice to Carolie and me, and gave us each a dime for pop!

Mom kept an eagle eye on us and insisted that we start getting ready for bed when it wasn't even dark. She said it was late. Muttering to each other, we complied, but peeked out the tent flap every once in a while. Late? For goodness' sake, another bunch of campers was just coming in to set up, on the other side of us. They were in such a hurry to get to the dance that they were just tying the tent corners to trees. Everybody got to go to the dance except us.

We weren't going to go to sleep, either! Who could sleep when the wonderful old-time dance music rang through the little campground? Of course, we were so played out from being in the water all day that our rebellion didn't last long and we dozed off in spite of ourselves.

All of a sudden, we woke to Mom's scared voice saying, "Who's there?" A head poked through the tent flap and said, "Hey, Jim, the cops are checking around. Better get rid of the empty beer bottles." Mother hissed indignantly, "There are no beer bottles here, full or empty. Get out of here, and right now!" He did.

We had nearly gone to sleep again when we heard scratchy noises. Someone was poking long poles into our tent! From her bed on the ground, Mom kicked the poles out again. They pushed in again and Mom pushed out again. In a louder hiss, she repeated, "Get out of here, and right now!" "Oh, sorry," someone said, and the poles disappeared.

Mom told us it was all right now and we should go back to sleep. We had just started to relax when somebody started to push the back tent pole into our pillows. Dad always set the back of the tent up against a tree and securely tied the top of it to the tree trunk in case of a high wind, and now somebody was trying to squeeze through that little space. This time I got into the act, too. Mom and I tried our best to hold the pole in place, and

Mom used her faithful line: "Get out of here, and right now!" It did no good.

Whoever was out there mumbled drunkenly, words that we kids knew about but would never have dared to mouth. With a mighty heave, he pushed his way between the tent and the tree. Then he made one more step right on to the gunny-sack-covered pit. He fell heavily, accompanied by the sound of smashing sealers.

He scrabbled around outside, his curses changing to a whining complaint about blankety-blank people who dig blankety-blank holes for poor people to fall into, and wandered off into the night.

We pushed the tent pole back into position with nervous laughter and finally went to sleep. That is, we youngsters did. Mom looked pretty worn out and kind of black under her eyes the next day. She gave Dad an extra hug when he showed up at about ten o'clock.

"Jim" turned out to be the pretty woman's partner, and later on they apologized nicely for warning the wrong tent. The people who had tied their tent up the night before apologized for trying to hide their tent poles in the wrong tent. The pretty woman offered to take Carolie and me to the rodeo grounds. Mom explained that we hadn't seen our dad for a while and should spend some time with him. Spend some time with Dad! We could do that every day, any day. But in spite of our agonized sign language behind the woman's back, we didn't get permission.

We did spend most of that day looking over everybody in camp, trying to guess who had fallen into the hole, but nobody confessed, and we never heard any more about it.

PLAYTIME

When there was time
to be a kid

We have a set of swings in the backyard and a couple of sturdy bikes and a playhouse, now crammed to the door with dolls, Lego, toy trucks, and tractors—items that my grandkids have mostly outgrown. We aren't about to get rid of the toys, as occasionally our honorary grandchildren, the neighbour kids, enjoy them. I suspect that they enjoy watching the cartoon channel or playing computer games more, though. Play has changed since I was a kid.

At country schools, recess and noon hour brought a couple of dozen children together to play, all ages, from five to sixteen or more. On weekends there was "visiting"—a sort of gathering of the clan, and the clan always included a bunch of kids. About the only way adults influenced our play was through our instinct to get someplace where they weren't so we didn't have to sit still and be quiet.

We played about six kinds of tag, including Poison Tag, where "it" had to chase the rest, holding the spot where she had been tagged; Shadow Tag, where your stepped-on shadow made you "it" and you were safe if you reached the shade of a building; and Squat Tag, where you were safe if you could squat before you were tagged. There were team games, such as Red Rover, Pom-pom Pullaway, Prisoners' Base, and Anti-eye-over (over the school barn, which had no windows to break). There were "one against the many" games, among them Mother May I, Simon Says, Hide and Seek, and its inverted variation, Sardines, where one kid hid and anyone who found him had to join him in the hidey-hole. The last one still looking was "it" next time round.

We skipped rope, when we could find one; we played hopscotch, tossing pebbles into a grid scratched in the dirt; we played Fox and Goose on a cut-pie shape tramped in the snow—I never did get the rules straight on that game; and we played London Bridge Is Falling Down, which always ended up in a tug-of-war.

And we played softball. My, how we loved playing ball. The big boys, Ken and Larry, were always the captains and always the pitchers—the starring positions. Everyone played. The more reliable were basemen and shortstops, and all the little kids ended up as fielders. The game went on at recess and noon-hour for a week at a time. If chicken-pox or colds reduced the teams too much, we played Scrub, where there were two batters at a time and field positions were rotated: shortstop went to third base, third baseman to second, and so on as each batter went out and was demoted to right field. Or we played five hundred. One kid hit the ball to the rest of us, who spread out and tried to catch it. A grounder was worth twenty-five points, first-bounce catch worth fifty, and if you caught a fly ball you got one hundred. Accumulating five hundred points gave you the chance to be batter.

Less organized pastimes included snaring gophers, tobogganing, skiing, skating on the dugout after a lot of shovelling snow off it, trying to ride the pigs or calves that ran loose in the barnyard, or sliding down haystacks. We swam in Dad's new horse water trough until we got too rough and sprang a seam in it. We climbed trees. We didn't always play safely. I once climbed high enough that the poplar top broke under my weight. Branches I hit on the way down probably saved my neck, but left me bruised and took off quite a bit of skin. A bunch of us found a ladder once and climbed to a granary roof to jump off onto the edge of a straw stack. The grownups caught us and stopped us before we broke any legs or arms or the granary roof.

Eileen Kopperud and friend Willie Thingvold with Shetland ponies

It was a real thrill while it lasted. We played house, tramping out rooms in the lush weeds, and once in Uncle Arvid's oat slough. I'm not sure he ever found out that we were the culprits or if he blamed the neighbour's cattle that occasionally broke in.

We had a lot of fun without expensive equipment or adult involvement. We learned a few things, too. We learned to take turns, to lose without whining and to win without grandstanding, to take our lumps and bruises and keep on trying. We learned that if we wanted to skate we had to shovel snow, and if we wanted the thrill of swooping downhill we had to climb to the top first. We learned co-operation, to stick together, and that tattling didn't pay. We burned calories and honed our physical reflexes.

We missed out, too—on expert coaching in organized sports; on dancing and skating lessons; on exposure to a world of other people, foreign countries, different ways of life. We knew the ways of gophers, coyotes, and badgers but never saw a llama or a lion. Art galleries, concerts, libraries—a world of culture taken for granted by today's generation—were denied us. We missed out on the magic world of computers. Today's youngsters seem to have inborn computer intelligence that our older brains cannot equal. We may have been more daring in some ways, but we're sure intimidated by bytes and bits.

Today's leisure opportunities far outnumber those in the "good old days," but too often kids haven't any spare time. Their lives are so clock-driven by lessons, practice, homework, and adult-inspired "worthwhile activities" that there isn't time to romp, to daydream, to be carefree. I even hear rumours that school recess is now considered dispensable and may be done away with. Poor kids.

Wouldn't it be nice if today's young could have all that is available today and still find the time and opportunity to have fun, maybe doing some of the "kid things" that their grandparents did so long ago?

WORDS AND MUSIC

*Why being my age
can pay off*

I hear that you can tell a person's age by the age of the
songs he knows. If that is true, my sister and I can claim
about twenty more years than we actually have because
we have engraved on our minds the lyrics of everything
from "K-K-K-Katie" and "Keep the Home Fires Burning" to
"Red Wing" from the early 1900s. We inherited the words
from our Dad, who was an excellent musician, and also
from Mom, who couldn't carry a tune in a basket but loved
music and knew the words to almost everything.

Music, both vocal and instrumental, was an important
part of family get-togethers. Grandma had a gramophone
(which we kids thought eminently logical), a little square
box with a removable silver handle to wind it with. Unless
there were grownups to help us, we were only allowed to
play one old record, "Hallelujah I'm a Bum" on one side
and "It Ain't Gonna Rain No More" on the other. In earlier
days, Dad and his brothers used to pay the "little kids" a
quarter to change records and keep the gramophone
wound up all evening while the older ones were learning
to play the new tunes on their instruments. They were
pretty well self-taught and played by ear, although they
could read music as well. Dad's fiddle, Uncle Jul's clarinet,
Uncle Garry's trumpet, and Albert Elton's guitar were
stored in the alcove under the stairs in Grandma's living-
room. (Albert was Dad's second cousin and sort of an honorary uncle.)

❖

Mom and Eileen and the Model T, 1927

It was a musical community. Nearly every church service in South Immanuel included a guest offering—a solo or duet, sometimes even a quartet. Mother often offered Carolie's and my services, and I suspect that a lot of the other solos and duets were also initiated by the performers' parents. We liked singing but learned early on never to look at Mother when we were on stage. She had such an expressive face and mouthed the words right along with us. If we happened to catch her eye, it was hard to concentrate on what we were supposed to be doing. A couple of incidents are impressed somewhere in my "when-I-was-a-kid" file—like my first solo when I was about four. I had to come on stage in my nightgown, holding a candle, to sing a lullaby to Baby Jesus at the church Christmas concert. The candle was okay, but I didn't much like the idea of parading around in a nightgown. I can't remember just what song it was, but I remember the nightgown and the candle part. And I remember Albert and his guitar, performing "The Letter Edged in Black" at an afternoon service. It is a very sad song and all about death, so I guess he thought it was appropriately religious.

Cars didn't have radios in those days, so we kids were encouraged to sing on longer trips—a way to keep peace in the back seat. Any time Carolie and I sang "M is for the Million" for Mom, we always followed it with "Silver Haired Daddy" for Dad, to keep peace in the front seat, we thought. It wasn't all that tactful: "O is only that she's growing old," when Mom was in her mid-thirties, and Dad, in his early forties, had about twenty years to go before his hair changed colour.

Dad occasionally joined in, but Mom usually just listened. In a bad snowstorm, or when the road was greasy and the Model T slithered around dangerously, Mom would nervously sing, sort of half under her breath, in her usual monotone. Dad teased her, saying that the singing didn't bother him, but he wished sometimes she would choose something other than "Nearer My God to Thee" as her theme song.

Copyright laws weren't applied as they are today. In

fact, many papers published the lyrics to popular songs and cowboy ballads on their young people's page. We school kids cut them out and pasted them in an old scribbler to add to our repertoire. We had good ears for music so the tunes were no problem. We learned the old classics: Stephen Foster spirituals, folk songs like "Men of Harlech" and "Greensleeves," as well as "The Maple Leaf, Forever" (all three verses) in school. When the war was on, we sang things such as "White Cliffs of Dover" and "I'll Be Seeing You" along with Vera Lynn and Gracie Fields on the radio.

So, I have a large collection of words and music on the shelves of my mental cupboard. The collecting seemed to end about halfway through the century. I am not sure why. Sometimes I think there is too much "Baby, Baby, Baby" in the often unintelligible lyrics, but then I realize that I know all the words to "Mairsey Doats" and "Free Widdle Fissies in an Iddy Biddy Poo," so it can't just be that I have instinctive taste. There have been lots of good songs since. Do you suppose my cupboard is full?

Oh well, with modern technology, I can hum along with anyone from Dolly Parton to Pavarotti, any time I feel the urge. And around a campfire, when everybody is humming the old, old songs—I really shine. After all, I know the words.

THE TORNADO

The barn took off,
the dog was demoralized,
the chickens lost their feathers,
and the kids enjoyed it all

When the spring thaw is over, we start watching reports of tornadoes, cyclones, and hurricanes on the weather channel. Last summer we were caught on the edge of a tornado that ripped through twenty-some miles of countryside east of us. We lost a couple of granaries, some shingles, and several shed roofs, but had nothing like the devastation that occurred around Spring Valley. When dark clouds start rolling overhead, we keep looking for stretchers—the long, whirling tails that just might develop into something serious. I take a lawn chair into the yard and stare at the sky, hoping that whatever is deciding to happen won't dare to happen if I'm watching it. Sometimes it works, sometimes not.

When I was about seven or eight, we had a tornado right in our yard, and I quite enjoyed it. It had been a hot, sticky afternoon, and about suppertime, clouds started to roll in from the west. All of a sudden, the air grew chilly and the wind started to howl. Mom called us kids inside and started shutting windows and doors.

Dad had finished milking, and after letting all the animals out of the barn, he hurried to the house with two pails of milk. The wind whirled clouds of dust around as we watched him. Mom opened the door for him and was about to shut it again when, to her surprise, Dad said, "Let it be." He set the milk down and went around opening the windows again. Then he said, "Look over toward Charlie Johnson's." A bit more than a mile away, a ragged, grey cloud stretched toward the ground. At the bottom of it was the father of all dust devils, whirling the soil up into the air.

Dad had grown up in Minnesota, where every farm had a cyclone cellar, and he recognized the devil wind coming our way. According to the wisdom of that time, if the eye of the cyclone passed close to the house, the vacuum created outside would cause the pressure inside the house to blow out the closed windows. He told us kids to stay away from the windows. However, he and Mom were too busy looking outside to notice that we figured a couple of feet was probably "away from the windows," so we got a pretty good look, too.

The noise was terrific; the wind whistled and roared like a freight train. Things started flying through the air—straw, boards, tree branches, parts of a hayrack. A wagon moved across the yard, chicken water pails went flying, and the dog, who had belatedly decided to move closer to the house, was lifted right up and over the row of lilacs. He cowered in the lee of the bushes, and as soon as we saw he wasn't hurt, my sister and I decided it was funny. Our laughter got our parents' attention, and we were sent away from the window.

The storm seemed a lot scarier when we weren't allowed to watch, but it was all over in a few minutes. After a brief spatter of rain, the sun came out and the wind stopped.

Dad went out to check the cattle. They were all right, but the rest of the farmyard was hardly recognizable. Both barns were gone, as were the chicken coop and the chickens. The damage was very erratic. The toilet had blown over, but the rickety old garage next to it was still standing. Two small wooden milkstools were sitting side by side where Dad had left them, just inside the barn door, but now there was no door—no barn, either. The house wasn't damaged except for a few missing shingles and a couple of bricks from the top of the chimney. (Dad found the bricks inside the chimney when he cleaned it in the fall.)

We were lucky to have escaped so lightly. The next couple of days were spent tidying up, looking for pails and other equipment, and bringing order out of chaos. The dog stayed very close to Dad and hid under the porch when Dad was in the house.

The chickens actually had the worst time of all. It took three or four days, but most of them found their way back to our yard. They emerged from the fields and ditches in twos and threes. Missing a lot of feathers, their backs sunburned fiery red, their feet sore, they were a bedraggled lot. They peered around here and there to make sure they had come to the right place and finally settled down under the lilacs, looking just a bit indignant at the whole affair.

A WEEK AT CAMP

*Bible camp, leaky tent,
swimming in the creek,
and cooking on a campstove*

When I asked my grandson how he had enjoyed Bible camp this summer, he said it was okay. The cabins and food were good; he liked canoeing and swimming; but it was pretty religious. They even had to pray before archery practice. Archery, canoeing, cabins—about the only word that I could relate to was "religious."

In 1941 Carolie and I, cousin Alvera, and friends Juverna and Hazel were allowed to spend a whole week at Simmie Bible camp. We'd been there before for one-day events: a Sunday morning service in the big tent, followed by a family picnic complete with fried chicken, summer sausage, dill pickles, buns, potato and jelly salads, cakes, cookies, aunts, uncles, cousins, grandpa, and grandma. After dinner we had to sit through another service with choirs and evangelists before we were free to play softball and get to know kids from other congregations. When the sun sank behind the hills, we were called in, dishevelled and sweaty, for a quick lunch of leftovers before heading home.

But 1941 was different. Dad and Uncle Arvid set up our old tent in a grassy nook, dug a little trench around it, and put old mattresses, blankets, and pillows along the back wall. Our mothers stored wooden egg crates full of food along the tent walls beside old suitcases that supposedly held enough clean clothing for a week, and they reminded us to keep one good outfit for next Sunday's services. Dad cautioned me to be very careful lighting the Coleman camp stove and to keep the gas can well away from the tent. Then they left. We were on our own. Well, sort of. The other campers were family groups, with a mother or aunt in charge, and I am sure they were keeping an eye on us.

We planned to be very methodical, preserving everything in a neat and tidy state. I had just turned fifteen and, as the oldest, did the camp stove cooking. We ate pretty well until the prepared food ran out. I remember frying potatoes, eggs, and bologna, as well as opening sealers of home-canned chicken or pork and beans.

We went swimming only once. Although I suppose everybody there had been to a public swimming beach at one lake or another, the "powers that be" at camp decided that it was not decent for boys and girls to swim together. The day after the boys had their swim, we girls put our bathing suits on under our other clothes and walked to the creek through the hot, dusty pasture, keeping a wary eye out for cows, and dodging cow-pies. Because the cows drank from the swimming hole, the "beach" was not tempting, but the water was warm and a joy after our trek. The women who chaperoned us sat on rocks under the hot sun, making sure that nobody drowned. They called it quits far too quickly for our liking. Soon we were summoned, donned shirts and slacks over our wet suits, and walked barefoot back to camp. Most of the mud on our feet and legs wore off on the way back.

One night it rained—hard—and our tent was patched here and there. Soon water dripped here and there, too. We shifted our blankets to drier spots. Then the dry spots became moist. The little trench, which was supposed to drain water away from us, overflowed and soaked the mattresses. It was a long night. We didn't need the wake-up bell next morning. We were already up bright and early, damply dressed, and had our blankets, mattresses, and some clothes draped over every bush and tree in the vicinity. We must have been pretty tough kids because the whole thing struck us as being hilarious.

Each day we attended morning chapel, two study sessions, choir practice, and evening service, so we got plenty of "religion," as my grandson expressed it. The rest of the time we climbed hills, played Red Rover and scrub softball, traded secrets, discussed our parents and our teachers, and generally enjoyed ourselves. We sponge-bathed in a wash basin, brushed our teeth behind the tent, and recycled our clothes, choosing the least soiled from the already worn pile as the week went by. We felt so free with none of the usual chores and no parents to answer to.

Next Sunday morning, with the expected arrival of our parents, we suddenly realized that we were living in shambles. We all got an attack of the tidies. By the time the day-trippers arrived, our blankets were folded, dishes and food put away, bits and pieces picked up, and trash all in the garbage. And miracle of miracles, although we may have been a bit wrinkled around the edges, we had each saved a clean set of clothing so we didn't disgrace the family. It had been a week to remember.

BARELY A DROP
TO DRINK

When water was
as precious as gold

The big rains have missed us again. Last spring we could hardly sneeze but it showered. Now we keep looking for the big, wet clouds and watch the wheat, which isn't looking too bad, considering. In the back of my mind, or maybe my heart, is the fear of drought.

Water was always a problem in the Thirties. Not only the lack of rain and the failed crops—those were the main problems—but water, just plain water, to wash in, to drink, to cook with, to swim in, or to fill the animals' drinking troughs. Our lives revolved around water.

Grandpa Kopperud moved from Minnesota to the Boule Creek district in 1912 ("Boule Creek" was considered more refined than the original name, "Bull Creek"). For about two weeks in spring, the snow melt filled the creek's steep banks and sometimes flooded the flat or even took out the wooden bridge, but the rest of the year it was just a series of small, stagnant pools. Not a reliable water source.

Wells were dug by hand or by horse-driven machines. There was a lot of talk about water-witching and rumours of people who were so good at it that they would tell someone to dig twenty feet from an existing dry hole and the water just came gushing in. This person never appeared in our district, I'm sorry to say, although we certainly had enough dry holes. Dad witched in our yard and dug a well where the forked twig pointed down. He did find water, but it trickled in so slowly that filling the horse trough exhausted it, and we'd have to wait several hours before enough seeped back for another troughful.

Dad optimistically installed a windmill over the well, and a heavy iron pump in it. One of our chores after school was to fetch two pails of water to fill the crock in the kitchen. It was easy to start the windmill. All we had to do was fasten two rods together and unhook a long lever that released the tail into the wind. Saskatchewan never lacked for wind. The stickler was that the pump had to be primed. One of us carefully dribbled a syrup pail full of water into the top of the pump to "wet up the leather" while the other one pumped the handle up and down until the leather valve seated itself and could suck up the water. After the first couple of gallons poured into the horse trough, we quickly replaced the long pipe with a pail. We were afraid we'd "lose the prime" if we took the time to hook up the windmill, so we both got on the pump handle and finished the job.

In a pasture about half a mile from the yard, there was a seepage well. When we went for the cows after school, we had to pump enough water for the cows before we brought them up. Although this was an easier pump to manage, it also had to be primed. My sister and her girl-friend once fooled around and spilled the priming water. Rather than trudge home for more priming water, they improvised and managed between the two of them to produce enough liquid to "wet the leather." Cows aren't too fussy.

Dad, Grandpa, and Uncle Jul made a dugout in the slough bottom of Grandpa's pasture. They loosened the soil with a disk and hauled it out with a scraper, a bucket affair dragged by two horses. The bucket had handles, and after the full scraper was far enough from the hole, the driver would flip up the handles and tip the bucket. They were lucky that the bottom was good clay. A sandy bottom would have meant a lot of wasted work, and they

Hauling water on the stoneboat.
(L to R) Mom, sister Betty, friend Linda, Dad, Star, and Oogie

never knew if the dugout would hold or not until they were done. Spring melt would fill the dugout, and rather than spread out over the whole slough and evaporate, the pool usually lasted all summer. (By the way, I astonished some Americans by telling them we swam in and skated on dugouts. To them, a dugout is a cyclone cellar.)

The dugout provided water for the animals, but we also used the good, soft dugout water for the house, hauling it with the stoneboat, which was a flat sled on wooden six-by-six-inch runners (I don't know why it was called a boat). We used the stoneboat in spring to pick stones from the field, first lugging them onto it, then hauling them to the rock pile and lugging them off. Dad also used it in winter to haul manure to spread on the fields. All summer, though, two barrels sat on it. We would pail the dugout water into them, cover them with old blankets so not too much water would slosh out, and slowly drive the team back to the house. On very hot days, my sister and I would lay claim to half a barrel of water and jump in for a swim.

Partly because water was hard to get, and partly because it had to be carried in and carried out again, it was well used. Laundry wash water was used to scrub out the toilet; the rinse water scrubbed the kitchen and porch and was then sprinkled on the flowerbed or the bushes. Dishwater was saved to wet down the chop for the pigs. Bathwater was used in turn, usually from the youngest to the oldest, with hot water added between each person. It was never settled among us kids if it was best to bathe first in just a little water, or wait and have the tub nearly full of used sudsy water. A shampoo required a basin and two pails, because after your hair was done, you washed the combs and brushes and then your or your mother's silk stockings. Then you washed up the bathroom floor—and the kitchen, too, unless it had just been washday.

When I grew up and got married, we hauled water for twenty-seven years before we finally got a good well with lots of water. My husband still doesn't really believe it won't run dry. I feel guilty about running water down the drain until it is nice and cold to drink, and I tend to get antsy when the kids and grandchildren have those long, long showers. I have overcome my qualms enough to fill my bath right to the overflow pipe. I lie there and soak and relax until even my feet have "dishpan hands." It's darned near as good as the barrel.

SALT AND SUCH

*Taking things with
a grain of salt is easier
than taking them with a lick*

Have you ever noticed that a train of thought is hard to derail? I started to think about salt a while ago. I have no idea why, unless it is because salt, along with coffee, bacon, cream, pie, and all the other things that make eating worthwhile are supposed to be bad for people, especially me.

I remember being fascinated in chemistry class when I found out that salt was really sodium chloride. Sodium is a metal so energetic that it is never found pure on earth. When it is made into the pure metal, it is so soft and waxy that it can be cut with a knife, so light that it will float on water. But that isn't such a great idea. It is so eager to react with oxygen that it pulls all the oxygen and half the hydrogen out of the water and forms lye, in the process getting hot enough to set fire to the remaining hydrogen. If the lye doesn't get you, the explosion will. Or the chlorine—a heavy, green gas so poisonous that it has been banned from use in warfare. Surely salt can't be as bad for you as its two elements.

There really isn't a scarcity of salt. Eons ago primeval rains washed the salt out of the earth into the ocean so enthusiastically that huge beds of it precipitated out onto the sea floor. Life began in the ocean's brine, and we still carry the traces. Our blood and the ocean have the same percentage of salt. We carry a bit of our life history around inside our skin.

When the earth was going through its growing pains, chunks of seabed salt were heaved out of the depths when continents moved around and mountains were being formed. The salt mines in central Europe, especially, have been used by man since prehistoric times and are still in use. Old tunnels in these mines were even used during World War II to cache stolen works of art.

Away from the ocean or a convenient mine, salt has always been expensive. The Roman legionnaires received part of their wages as salt. In the lands they occupied they could trade salt for other necessities of life. The Latin word for salt, *sal*, is where we get the word salary—and makes sense of the expression "not worth his salt."

The Bible has quite a bit to say about salt besides the turning of Lot's wife into a pillar of it. I sometimes wonder if she didn't look back on purpose. Lot doesn't strike me as good husband material or much of a father, either. In addition to Mrs. Lot's story, there are expressions like "salt of the earth" and "salt losing its savour and being thrown into the street and trod underfoot" in the Bible, too. In those days, salt was usually chiselled in chunks from dry lake beds, and often the blocks contained quite a bit of clay. Sometimes the blocks were more clay than salt and were useless for preserving food—the salt had lost its savour. I suppose the clay made good street material, and they didn't need the salt there anyway—streets rarely got icy in Palestine. Even today in parts of the world like the western Sahara, camel caravans are loaded with blocks of salt from dry lake beds to be sold many miles away in cities like Timbuktu.

There must be dozens of sayings that involve salt. Sitting below the salt in medieval times meant that you weren't very important. Throwing spilt salt over your shoulder chased the devil away. Dad told us that if we shook salt on a bird's tail, it couldn't fly, and we could pick it up. The same thing was said about rabbits. Mind you, we kids had that all figured out before we wasted much time running around with a salt shaker. Speaking of salt shakers, the world's biggest and ugliest sits beside Number 2 highway south of Moose Jaw, a bin for salt and sand when the roads are icy.

Salt lore was part of our childhood. Plant-eating animals crave salt. Wild deer will go to salt licks around alkali sloughs and lick the salty mud. Porcupines will chew axe handles just to get at the residue of salt from sweaty hands, and were even known to chomp up the seats of old wooden privies if the door was left open. Pork was rubbed with a mix of salt, saltpetre, and liquid smoke to make home-cured bacon and ham; beef chunks were put in brine to make corned beef. Cabbage was chopped into crocks with salt sprinkled between the layers to make sauerkraut. Dad was a firm believer in soaking an angry, infected cut in hot salt water to draw out the poison. A little cotton bag filled with salt was heated in the oven and laid on our pillow to ease the pain of earache.

Nowadays there are salt blocks of all kinds and colours—red, pink, blue, and sort of purple; blocks complete with trace minerals for cattlemen to use to keep their animals healthy. When Carolie and I were young, Dad always used to put a big white block of salt in the barnyard for the cows and horses. They really enjoyed licking it. I know why. It tasted great. When nobody was looking we kids gave it a lick ourselves. We were particular, though. We never licked the dirty looking part—just the places that the cows had already cleaned off with their tongues.

HAYWIRE

*Don't underestimate
the power of
a little haywire*

Blue sky overhead, bright sun, sturdy arms lifting fragrant hay onto a horse-drawn rack. Sounds idyllic, doesn't it? Well, it might if you never had to do it. The reality was hot sun, no shade, sweaty palms on a fork that weighed a ton by eleven in the morning, itchy hay in your hair and down your neck, and about five more loads to go before quitting time, not to mention that the whole works also had to be unloaded and tramped into a stack that was dense enough to shed rain. No wonder balers became popular.

The first baler used wire ties about nine or ten feet long with a loop in one end. It was still pretty labour-intensive, needing three people to operate it: one to drive the tractor, another on one side to move the ledger plate and thread wire, and a third to poke the wire ends through the loop and twist-tie the compressed bale. On the plus side, the workers could sit down on the job! Also, the baler made hay a shippable commodity. During the Dustbowl years, prairie farmers had to buy, or sometimes get through relief, bales of hay from the east to feed their animals. That's when they discovered haywire.

We don't know much about real haywire now. The word is used to describe something that's mixed up, gone awry, a poor fix, kooky. Back then, when the bales were pulled out of the storage pile, pulled apart, and fed to the animals,

Coffee time for the threshing crew was a welcome break.

the discarded wires were usually looped over a convenient fencepost. It didn't take long for resourceful farmers to find a multitude of uses for the wire. Money was too scarce to buy proper repair parts, so haywire was used to mend a broken barbwire fence, to fasten loose bits and pieces onto machinery, and to splice broken harnesses in the busy season until there was time to do it up right. A broken pitchfork handle could be splinted and wired together to give a few more months of use. Seals, bearings, o-rings—anything with convenient holes—were strung together with haywire and hung on a nail in the shed in case they could be reused. Dad used haywire to tie the old canvas tent into a compact roll and hang it from a rafter out of reach of mice. He wrapped an old glass vinegar jug with a gunny sack and secured it with haywire. When the sacking was soaked in the morning, it kept drinking water cool all day in the field. We kids used haywire to make toy machinery and to tie laths together when making a rack for our small wagon. One of our neighbours even used it to keep loose fenders from leaving his old car entirely. Haywire was not elegant but it was useful indeed.

Useful as it was, it was still considered a poor fix. I remember one of our neighbours scornfully remarking to my dad that if haywire ever disappeared, the farmer across the road would have to quit farming. We have its equivalent today: duct tape. Can't you just hear a young fellow, fifty years from now, saying, "The whole machine just went duct tape, so I left it in the corner of the pasture."

GRASSHOPPERS

Why John the Baptist was braver than Samson

When I was a child, I always thought that John the Baptist was the bravest man in the Bible. Gideon may have been a mighty warrior, taking his little band against a superior army while armed only with empty pitchers, torches, and trumpets. He, however, required a couple of favourable fleecy omens before he would even start out. Samson, that big bully, tied little foxes' tails together and set fire to them. Some hero! He would have been thumped good for cruelty to animals if my mom had been anywhere around! Joshua and Caleb must have felt pretty sheepish when they had to ask a woman to let them sneak out her back window, and please would she get a basket and lower them carefully on a rope? But John the Baptist, wow! John ate grasshoppers.

On the Saskatchewan prairie, we knew grasshoppers well. I remember clouds of them darkening the sky, their chittering wings sounding like rain on a tin roof. We used to hold them up by their back legs and look them straight in the eye and say, "Grasshopper, grasshopper, spit tobacco juice or I will pull your head off." They always spit. Then we stepped on them.

Leaping hoppers used to drive their heads into the little honeycomb openings in car radiators, and the red, green, yellow, and blue wings made a beautiful mosaic to adorn the sombre black or navy Fords and Chevs. The mosaic also made the radiator heat up and boil over. If a kid rode with her head out the car window to get a bit of breeze, a flying hopper could nearly put her eye out. They had scratchy legs and were forever getting down the necks of our shirts. Our parents hated them because they destroyed crops and gardens. Oh, we knew them. But we didn't eat them. John the Baptist ate them with wild honey. The very thought made our throats raspy.

I did hear once that John's locusts weren't insects but a kind of pod that grew on a tree. I knew this couldn't be true. Imagine, trees growing out in the desert. What nonsense. I knew that my John just grabbed those hoppers by their back legs, dipped their heads in honey, and chomped them down. He was brave.

Several years ago, a newspaper story told of a prairie farmer who had invented a machine that could gather up swarms, nay, veritable hordes of these little beasties, after which he would slay them instantly in a vat of hot water, from whence they could be exported to the Orient to serve as snacks. They could be salted and deep fried, or covered with chocolate. The scratchy hind legs would have to be removed first, of course. I haven't heard much about that lately, although it did sound like a good idea. Probably couldn't find anybody to take off all those legs!

A CALCULATING MIND

How not to speak metric

My generation, and to some extent the baby boomers as well, was raised on ounces and pounds, pints and gallons, inches and feet, square yards and acres. Along with the times tables, we were forced to memorize most of the other arcane systems of measurement that were printed on the backs of our exercise books. (We weren't allowed to call them scribblers because we were not supposed to scribble.) About the only measurement we can take for granted now is time. Sixty minutes still form an hour and 365¼ days add up to a year, even if time doesn't fit into the metric system.

We were assured by our elders that "a miss is as good as a mile" and "an ounce of prevention is worth a pound of cure," and our ritual birthday paddling was concluded with a "pinch to grow an inch." My grandson thinks that my old-fashioned expressions are quaint and sweet, but really, we speak two different languages when it comes to measurement. If I tell him I came within two feet of hitting something with the truck, he doesn't have a clue how narrowly I escaped. If I need an eighteen-inch board, I ask him to find one as long as the distance from his elbow to his fingertips. Oh, I can do simple metric conversions in my head, but sometimes it's just too much bother to do the math. I figure if I have to be bilingual in measurement, everybody else should, as well.

It gets serious when it comes to chemicals. Most farm chemicals are poisonous, and we approach them with trepidation. Some do-gooder decided to force us all into the logic of metrification and decreed that instructions for herbicides, fungicides, and insecticides be labelled only in litres and hectares. Our land is measured in acres; we think in ounces and quarts; our sprayers are calibrated in gallons. So we convert. We change litres and millilitres into quarts and ounces, multiply hectares by 2.4 to get acres, and do the math. The possibility of error is extreme, and so are the consequences of error with potent chemicals. Surely there is room on the label of agricultural poisons for both metric and ounces per acre for us old guys.

Metric isn't all bad, though. Have you ever noticed that we get places faster in Canada than in the States? And I'm not talking about the fifty-five-mile-per-hour speed limit on some of the highways down south, although conscientious Canadians like my husband seem to be the only drivers who obey the speed limit. Everything zooms past us, whether it's a semi or an old rattletrap held together with spit and hope. No, I think the distance signs create the time warp. When you see one that says "Minot—45," it means nearly another hour's drive, but if the sign says "Saskatoon—45," we get there in less than thirty minutes.

THE THUNK UNDER THE STAIRS

Something's out there ...

I have a very agile mind. I can believe in two definitely opposite things at the same time. Take, for instance, the scientific theories of evolution and Bible stories. Or the conviction that Canada is the best and freest of countries—and is run by incompetents and under the heel of multinational corporations.

Well, I don't believe in ghosts or bogeymen, either, but if I ever see one, I'll set a new track record for grandmas.

One evening long ago, after chores and supper dishes were done, our family was sitting around the living-room listening to the radio. Dad asked me to go down to the basement and bring up some apples. We didn't have electric lights then, and the flashlight batteries were dead, so I was given three wooden matches for the trip: one to see me down the steps, one to find my way around down there, and one to light my way back upstairs.

Our basement steps had open risers. In the space behind them, Mom kept empty cardboard boxes and other useful stuff. That's also where I imagined something could be lurking, ready to reach between the steps and grab my ankles some dark night. I knew better, but, as I say, I have always had an agile mind.

The first match got me down the steps safely, but when I struck the second one on the cement wall, it broke and the head fell off, still unlit. The third one lasted long enough for me to find the apple box, grab five apples, and make it back to the foot of the stairs. I could see only a faint glimmer of light at the top through the open basement door.

Then I heard the *thing*! In the silence and gloom, it was breathing with hoarse, gasping sounds, and every couple of seconds there was a thunk-thunk, like a very slow heartbeat. I told myself firmly that it must be my imagination, but I knew it wasn't.

I tried to call for help but couldn't make any sounds come out. After what seemed an eternity, I rushed at the stairs and scrambled up, expecting at any second to feel a cold, wet hand grasp my ankle.

When I burst into the living-room, Dad took one look at my white face and trembling limbs. He listened to my incoherent story, and rather than scoff, "Don't be silly," he said, "Let's go see." He led me to the top of the stairs, where I stood rooted while he went down. Then he said, "I do hear something," and smiled. He took me out the kitchen door and pointed to Old Pup, who was lying in the moonlight beside the partly open basement window.

Old Pup had apparently just come back from a great chase after something or other in the course of his duty to keep the yard free of real or imagined intruders. He was catching his breath, water dripping from his panting tongue, and complacently swishing his tail back and forth against the basement wall—thunk-thunk, thunk-thunk.

I was immensely relieved, although it did take a while to get back to an ordinary frame of mind. We ate the apples, went to bed, and there I reviewed the evening. I reflected that although it was Old Pup making the noises then, it might not *always* be just Old Pup. I would be careful, especially going down the cellar steps in the dark.

There is nothing under those steps now; my childhood home was sold and moved. All that's left in the old farm-yard is a concrete foundation around a depression nearly filled with rusty iron and old fenceposts. When we

CURLS AND SUCH

*Straight hair and Dad's
barbering was bad enough;
then we discovered curls*

Does anyone else hate those smug females who flaunt their hair on television? Every evening, sometimes three or four times in the same hour, some gorgeous blond, brunette, or redhead swishes her long tresses hither and yon, mangles them with her hands, dangles her head upside down, and extols some magic potion that is responsible for her glorious mane. I can tell you what would happen if I used the exact same product and dared to swish, mangle, and dangle. I would look as if I'd just got out of bed, and had spent most of the night with my head under the pillow, at that.

Hair has undergone a lot of abuse through the ages. Cleopatra shaved hers all off and wore a wig—so we are told. Dark Roman and Greek women envied the tow-headed Franks (even though they called them barbarians) and bleached their own hair with a caustic mix that included ashes of manure as well as other equally tasteful ingredients. Women attending the French court of Louis, the Sun King, had model ships and other feats of engineering and architecture built into their coiffures—and slept on neck rolls so that the towering edifices would last for several weeks. Queen Elizabeth I shaved the front part of her head because high foreheads were in vogue. In the late 1800s, when people became more concerned about cleanliness and didn't accept bedbugs, lice, and fleas as inevitable facts of life, pioneer women shaved their boys' heads if they came home from school with a case of lice. Mindful of Saint Paul, who decreed that a shorn woman was shamed, they subjected their daughters to a head soaked with kerosene, which was wrapped tightly for hours, then a shampoo and a painstaking procedure with a fine-tooth comb to get rid of the nits—louse eggs that had been cemented to the base of hairs close to the scalp.

My sister Carolie and I were born late enough not to have to undergo anything like that. We both had milk-white, stubbornly straight, fine hair. Every couple of weeks Dad sat us on a board laid across the arms of a wooden chair and trimmed up our Dutch bobs: bangs on the forehead and the rest cut off at ear-lobe level. With every breath, we sniffed in itchy particles of hair, and we hated the "clippers on the neck" part. It all seemed to take so long, and we really didn't know if Dad was serious when he said if we wiggled he might accidentally cut off our ears. On Sunday mornings when we got into church, he would clamp us each in turn between his knees to straighten parts and undo the tangles we had acquired since leaving home.

When we grew old enough to notice that some people had curls, Carolie and I decided to get some, too. Woolworth's in Swift Current sold three little metal curlers on a card for ten cents. We each anted up a nickel and shared. One morning I would have two little sausage shapes, one over each ear, and Carolie had one; the next morning I had one and she had two. Mom let us go to school like that. She knew very well that in an hour or so our hair would be as straight as bones again.

When I was fourteen, I spent a weekend helping a neighbour with a large family, a bad leg, and a new baby. With the five dollars I made, I got my first permanent. My hair was sectioned off into little rectangles; each fastened in a little rubber vice. Then a nose-tingling, ammonia-smelling lotion was applied and the strand rolled onto metal rods that snapped into the rubber vices. A tall machine, with many clamps at the ends of thick electric cords all hanging from a halo-like circle, was rolled over to my chair, and a

(L to R) Eileen, Baby Carl, and Carolie, 1935

metal clamp was put on each roll of hair. Then the power was switched on. The smell was awful, the whole thing tremendously heavy, and I was scared to pieces. After what seemed like hours but was probably only fifteen minutes, I was dismantled, shampooed, and released from custody. My head felt so light (my neck felt as if it had regained several inches lost under the weight of the hairdo contraption), my hair was still attached to my head, and it was *curly*.

Over the years, my hair turned from white to blond, with occasional intervals of darker shades thanks to little bottles that come in boxes, and now it's back to white again. I learned to sleep with metal curlers first, then to make pincurls, an every-night chore. I tried home permanents for a while and am now back again to salon permanents, although they should really be called temporaries in my case.

With the help of pincushion rollers, conditioner, mousse, and hairspray, I can manage to look presentable. But no matter what I use, I cannot swish, mangle, or dangle a luxurious mane like the models do. I secretly suspect they have pulled a Cleopatra and in real life are all as bald as eggs. Well, perhaps not, but at least the idea makes me feel better.

NUMBER, PLEASE

*Central was a lady, a general
ring meant "fire," and everybody
rubbered, but no one admitted it*

Telephones have been around longer than I have, and nearly every family had a telephone when I was little. Batteries and the mechanics were encased in an oak cabinet, about twice the size of a shoebox, fastened to the wall. It was usually near enough to the kitchen table that whoever sat beneath would crack the top of his head when getting up. You turned a black crank on the right to ring the bells that sat like eyes on the front; you talked into a cone-shaped thing below the bells; and you listened with a black Bakelite receiver that was attached to the box by a cord and hung from the switch-arm on the left side. Our ring was "line 7 ring 31," which translated into three long turns on the crank and one short turn. To phone anyone not on our neighbourhood line we had to contact "Central" in Cadillac by pushing a little button while ringing. She would plug in the cables that connected two lines and ring the number on the other line. Her headphone made it possible for her to monitor the call and disconnect the lines when we finished talking, although we were also supposed to ring off to indicate the line was clear.

Central, as she was generally called, had to be very discreet, as she became privy to pretty well everything that went on in the whole district. Party-line subscribers were usually quite discreet anyway, as their conversation was available to anyone on that same line who lifted the receiver. This was called rubbering. No one ever admitted to doing it, but everyone did. First you had to shush everyone in the room, then seal the cone with the palm of your free hand to muffle any stray noise, then lift the receiver gently so it didn't make a click. Rubbering could be entertaining and useful but was usually mundane. One woman hotly denied ever rubbering but she kept her kitchen clock on top of the phone and its tick double-crossed her. It was a fairly innocent diversion, and in case of accident or illness, neighbours quickly brought help, even if they never explained how they knew it was needed.

One extra-long ring on the party line meant a general ring from the Central switchboard. Everyone was supposed to listen. Sometimes it was only the arrival of a long-awaited railcar of coal or apples to be distributed for drought relief, or notice of a coming Sports Day, but often it was a call for help in fighting a prairie fire ignited by sparks from the train, and quite a few times to get help to fight a fire right in Cadillac. Cadillac kept trying to burn itself up, or down, or whatever.

Our district managed to keep our telephone system alive during the Depression, but several local phone companies went broke. Prairie ingenuity took over. Farmers ran barbed wire on insulators along their fencelines and connected the neighbourhood, making use of the company's now-discarded telephone boxes. It was probably illegal, but it could save lives in case of a blizzard, accident, or illness, and at the very least no doubt saved the sanity of many an isolated farm woman.

Now the party lines are gone, so nobody rubbers anymore. Many trunk lines have been laid underground, so we don't even have to manoeuvre machines around telephone poles in the field. We can call up practically anywhere in the world. I'm even deciding if I want to launch myself on the Internet. Our kids all have it and they keep telling me that I need it, too. I feel as if I'm being dragged, kicking and screaming, into an electronic world where I'm not sure I want to go. A phone in the computer room would be handy, though, so my husband, Ev, is tracing wires to see where another jack can be installed.

Only a few problems remain to be solved: the intrusion of telemarketers, as well as the irritating telephone menus that confuse me with instructions to push this or that. On general principle, I always push the number that summons a human, any human. Most of all, I resent the frustration of being put "on hold" to listen to bland music interspersed with blander voices telling me how important my call is to them, while my long-distance bill keeps getting bigger and bigger. With party lines and the Central operator, we used to have more live humans on the line that we really wanted; now I can't even get one.

THE ROAD TO SCHOOL

The two-mile trip to school
was seldom boring

My kids rode to school in a long, yellow bus. They got on about a quarter to eight and came home again nearly nine hours later. A lengthy day, especially for little ones. I'm not sure they had it better than we did in the Thirties. We usually walked the two miles, winter or summer, although when we grew older and the horses weren't needed in the field, we took a rig.

When we were small, our folks sometimes made arrangements for us to ride with the Lambert kids, who lived a mile and a half farther from school than we did. Mr. Lambert had built seats along the sides of a light wagon for his large family—eventually nine of them all going at the same time. Of course, kids often fight and are sometimes mean. I often got on my high horse and walked home. Carolie didn't feel insulted so easily, so she usually rode. Maybe she just didn't want to walk.

We envied the kids who walked to school barefoot in summer. Mom made us wear shoes. I remember occasionally hiding my shoes in a culvert just over the hill from our house and putting them back on before I reached home. Some of the kids had to go barefoot from early spring to late fall—they simply had no shoes to wear. One youngster's feet were so chapped and cracked that he sometimes left bloody footprints on the school floor. One of the advantages of wearing shoes was that we could stomp on the big, black carrion beetles that pranced down the trail. We had to hold our noses when we passed their remains on the way home because they smelled truly horrible by then.

We didn't waste much time on the way to school—we would never be excused for being late, and anyway, as soon as we got there, we played softball until the bell rang. A couple of times, though, as we came over the top of Grandpa's hill, we saw Uncle Jul walking from Grandpa's house to do chores at his new farm across the road. As soon as he saw us, he started to clown around. He would walk clumsily, fall over his feet, crawl a couple of yards, sit and scratch his head, then roll for a few feet. As we shrieked with laughter, he would get up, walk backward, and generally just act like an idiot, all the time pretending not to notice us at all.

On the way home, we often cut through Grandpa's pasture, which usually took a while. We picked lunchpails full of crocuses to take home to Mom. They were often wilted and full of ants, but she always arranged some of them in a little bouquet for the supper table. And we snared gophers, using binder twine that every kid always had tucked somewhere on his or her person. We used our lunchpails to fetch water from the nearby slough to pour down the main gopher hole. We always closed the other holes with dirt so the gopher couldn't sneak out the back door. On calm days we fought the mosquitoes that swarmed around our heads until we could hardly breathe. We knew they carried equine encephalitis, a sleeping sickness that horses get, and we wondered if we might not get it, too.

When we became old enough to drive, Dad sometimes let us take Spark Plug and Queen with the cart in summer or the cutter in winter. Carolie and I had to unhook them, take off their bridles, and stable them in a stall in the school barn. At lunchtime, one of us had to feed them the oat sheaf Dad had sent along. After school, we always raced to see whose team and rig would be first out of the gate. Carolie and I often won, not only because we were pretty good, but also because Dad always saw to it that our harness was in good shape. Lots of the kids had to fix broken straps and loose buckles before they could hitch up. Spark Plug and Queen were placid, reliable animals, so much so that when it was cold and windy, we just hunched under the robe, peeking out now and then to see where we were. In fact, once we hadn't even hooked the reins to the bridles and didn't realize it until Dad told us after he had put the team in the barn. The horses probably knew the road better than we did, anyway.

We were about eight and ten when Mom borrowed Mrs. Lambert's pattern and made us sunhats. They were made of colourful, cool cotton with wide brims and a circle of haywire inserted all the way around the edge to keep them from flopping in our faces. One day on our walk home from school, Carolie and I went through Grandpa's yard and stopped off at his outdoor toilet. We don't remember now who accidentally knocked the other's sunhat down through the third hole, but the other one then threw the remaining hat down in retaliation. Suddenly we realized that we were both in serious trouble. So we told Grandma what we had done. Grandpa fished them out with the hoe; Grandma washed them and gave us a good scolding. They stood together watching our progress through the pasture, and I am quite sure they were laughing. They didn't tell on us, either. Mom never found out till years later when we told her ourselves.

Carolie and I often sang as we walked; in fact, that's where we taught ourselves to harmonize. We daydreamed, shared confidences, learned to persevere even when we were tired or too hot or too cold. We fought and made up, and became as close as sisters can be. The road to school was a great teacher.

No, I don't envy the kids who have to take the school bus every day. Bus kids may not have to fight the sun or the wind or the mosquitoes the way we did, but just the same, they miss a lot of good things we enjoyed on the road to school.

PEN AND INK

Pen nibs, penmanship,
and an ink-stained floor

A Velveeta cheese box nearly full of ballpoint pens sits in my top desk drawer. A lot of them have just about had it and should be tossed, but when I last went through them, they all had a little ink left, maybe not enough to complete a signature, but who can tell? If a pen can scribble a couple of circles when I check it out, back into the box it goes. I hate to throw away a ballpoint that still writes, probably because of the grief that straight pens used to give me when I was a kid at school.

After Grade Four, we used pencils for arithmetic only. A straight pen was a milestone on the road to maturity. We could hardly wait for the day when we were big enough to use one. It was beautiful when new: a brightly lacquered rod about the size and shape of a chopstick, with a white, ridged rubber finger grip near the thick end. Removable nibs were two for a nickel, so we usually started the term with two new nibs. The idea was that we would dip the pen into the ink just far enough to cover the little hole at the top of the slotted point. The nib would pick up a small drop of ink, enough to write several sentences in fine copperplate penmanship, and then it was back to the ink bottle for another drop. In nearly every school there was one pupil, usually a girl, who could actually accomplish this and make the rest of us look like slobs. We had one of those.

Grade Four students are not noted for motor control. And when a kid was growing as quickly as I was, Grades Five, Six, Seven, and Eight didn't show much improvement. All grades took penmanship for fifteen minutes every day. From the Palmer Penmanship text, the teacher would copy the day's task onto the blackboard. First came several lines of O's linked into a running coil, then a series of up-and-down strokes like close-set picket fences with an elegant arched tail to finish them off. After that came the letter of the day, in capital and small script, and then words containing the letter. Everything was supposed to sit on the line and extend to precisely the right height.

I always started with honourable intentions, for all the good that did. Hold the pen at the wrong angle and the nib would stick on the up-slope, spattering everything already written. Use a smidgen too much pressure and that little drop of ink that was supposed to last and last descended all at once and made a blot. Nothing that I wrote sat on the line for more than an inch, and I never did get the hang of that little arched tail at the end. At least I was not alone in my failure. Everyone else had a messy writing book, too, except for Little Miss Perfect.

Pen nibs were delicate. They were slightly flexible and were supposed to shape their tip to a slant compatible with one's individual style. As most of us had no style at all, they just became individually deformed at our school. Dropping a pen, point down, on the floor or using it to re-ink the carvings left on the desktop by our predecessors didn't help, either.

The rest of the pen didn't fare much better. After a couple of weeks, the white rubber finger grip was ink-stained and tattered. The bright lacquer stem had tooth marks on the end and was sometimes chipped right down the whole length. Mine always looked like that, and for the life of me I can't remember even putting it in my mouth.

Thank goodness, the squat ink bottles were nearly unbreakable. Our desks were slanted, and ink bottles made a habit of inching toward the edge. We were all aware of that and tried our best to keep them top centre, but every week one or two hit the deck. It is amazing how far and fast a little bit of ink can spread. Then there was a scramble to wipe it up and wash off as much of the stain as we could.

Actually, the blotters were the best part of using a straight pen and ink. Several times a year, the CCM bicycle company would send us a supply, white or green, pink or pale blue on the working side, but with glowing red or royal blue bikes on the glossy front. (That's about as close as any of us came to having new bikes, too.) On a boring, hot afternoon, when the flies buzzed around sleepily in the windows and your bare legs stuck to the seat with sweat, it was kind of interesting to drop little beads of ink onto the blotter and watch the dark circles spread and join.

You just cannot do that with a ballpoint pen. But you can't splatter or blot, or spill all the ink out onto the floor, either. I guess that is why I have a whole boxful of ballpoints in my top desk drawer.

THE ODOUR
OF LEARNING

Memories of chalk dust,
orange peel, and Dustbane

There is definitely something missing from the pioneer museum's replica of a one-room school. The fold-up seats, screwed onto one-by-fours in long rows, look right; the beat-up teacher's desk with textbooks and a brass bell on top, the shallow drawer pulled out to show the "register," and the strap are authentic enough; there are the oak-framed portraits of King Edward and Queen Alexandra, or of King George V and his Mary, and perhaps a sepia print of Rosa Bonheur's "Horse Fair," or Gainsborough's "Blue Boy." There is the octagonal pendulum wall clock with Roman numerals on its face and the fancy black hands that seemed to move so slowly on stuffy afternoons. Yet to those of us who sat up straight on the fold-up seats, or reigned behind the teacher's desk, something vital is missing. It's the distinctive smell: a combination of chalk dust, stale orange peelings, and cedar-scented Dustbane. Someone really should invent a spray can with that combination for museum use. I might even buy a can for old times' sake.

We used to have blackboards that were black, not those dark green ones they call blackboards today. Along the top, the teacher used coloured chalk to outline a flowery border, following faint marks that chalky brushes left in the pinholes in the stencil, or if she were artistic, an entire alphabet, capitals and small, in both print and writing, with a little picture for each letter: an apple for A, a boy for B, a cat for C, and so on. All written work left a couple of inches' clearance for the border, and if some kid, as an overly enthusiastic blackboard monitor, accidentally swooshed the eraser too high and wrecked the border, he was immediately demoted to scrubbing out the washbasin or clapping blackboard erasers outside in a cloud of chalk dust.

We always had morning exercises, although we just stood around, so we didn't really see where the "exercise" part came in. We stood beside our desks, at attention, to sing "O Canada" and recite the Lord's Prayer. Then we sat down, splayed our hands on the desk on top of a handkerchief, and were checked for clean hands and fingernails as the teacher walked up and down the aisles, asking about toothbrushing and such things. She was fairly lenient, as she knew many of us had walked a couple of miles to school or else hitched and unhitched horses to the school cart, and our hands were seldom squeaky clean. One of my schoolmates always had a clean hanky for inspection, ironed and folded, in his back pocket. His well-used sleeve ensured that one handkerchief lasted him for morning inspection for months. When I started to teach, I found out that the trip up and down the aisle, under the guise of a fingernail inspection, was actually a check for head lice, ringworm, or impetigo that could spread through the class like wildfire.

School supplies were Spartan. In the fall, each student was expected to bring a pencil, an eraser, eight notebooks, a straight pen and several nibs, a ruler, crayons, and a pencil box. Every fall, I made up my mind that this year I would not dog-ear or blot my scribblers, chew my pencil, drop my pen on the floor, nor peel the paper off my crayons. And each year, after a month or so, my exercise books were dilapidated, my pencil bore teeth marks, my pen nibs were scratchy and sputtered blots here and there, and my naked crayons lay in stubby bits. The school board supplied foolscap for exams and heavy white paper for art. It was doled out in six-by-nine-inch sheets for art period Friday afternoons. Without fail, the first art period each year was spent drawing and pencil-shading the teacher's bell. There must have been some law about it! I got so sick of drawing lopsided bells and trying to put in highlights when I wasn't even sure what a highlight was.

The school board also bought a tall glass bottle of blue-black ink, to be meted out into the half-moon inkwells with flippy lids that sat in the top right corner of the big kids' desks. This purchase was discontinued after the big ink bottle was left on the top shelf in the storeroom through an unheated weekend when everything liquid froze solid. The ink bottle shattered and, the next time the furnace was lit, cascaded ink down onto the art paper and foolscap. After that, we had to get an individual ink bottle that kept jumping off the desk for no reason at all. A scrub cloth and pail stood in the corner of the back entry, and sooner or later, we all learned to use them.

Ink blotters were free, donated by the CCM company, with beautiful pictures of sleek, new bicycles on the back. The Neilson company donated a map of Canada on a wind-up roller, complete with big pictures of chocolate bars poised over Alaska, Greenland, Oregon, and Massachusetts. They looked so yummy. The Wheat Pool occasionally provided ugly orange exercise books with a stiff wheat sheaf on the front cover, and on the back, as on all the other exercise books, multiplication tables up to 12 times 12, plus other useful tables for calculating quarts and gallons, drams and grams, feet, chains, rods, roods and acres, barrels and tuns, and something abbreviated CWT, a one-hundred-pound measure that we called "cutwait."

And then there was Plasticine or, as we knew it, "plastercine." Although it started out red and green, plastic, and oily-smelling, it soon degenerated into a hard, streaky grey lump that had to be massaged for ten minutes before it would even roll into a cylinder. Only the beginners were really entitled to use it, but we older kids with stronger hands got a chance to fiddle with it when we were supposedly helping the little ones.

In August my grandkids go shopping for school supplies with a page-long list: felt markers, special glue, scissors, binders, and other exotic things, plus they take nearly thirty dollars to school for workbooks and stuff. It is a wonder we learned anything with the meagre bits that the teachers and we had to work with. And yet we did. I can't think of anybody who left our school unable to read, write, and do arithmetic. Our parents and teachers expected no less. On the other hand, when I read about the new discoveries on how environment influences learning ability, I sometimes think that our brains may have been subtly programmed to learn by the smell of chalk dust, old orange peelings, and Dustbane.

THE DAY OF THE
FOUR-LEGGED HOPPERS

My first day of teaching

My first day as a teacher was daunting. If I could have thought of any way to get out of it, it might also have been my last day. However, I had signed a contract and burnt my bridges, so that was that.

I started early to walk the mile and a bit from my boarding house, past ripened fields to the top of a gravelly hill. There, a two-acre fenced schoolyard held a boxy schoolhouse, white with green trim, a low red barn, and two red outhouses standing like sentinels, one in each far corner. At least they had once been red, white, and green, but it had been a long time since the paint, or anything else, was new. The schoolroom floor was so worn that the diagonal sub-floor showed through here and there. The blackboards were chipped and shiny, the plastered walls cracked and grimy. A string of stove-pipes snaked across the ceiling from the jacketed coal heater in one corner to the chimney in the opposite one. Wire slings fastened to nails in the ceiling kept them aloft.

Although I realized that the school's shabbiness was the result of the long depression of the Dirty Thirties, followed by wartime austerity, it was still shabby. Four years of war had also caused a severe shortage of teachers, which was why I, barely past my eighteenth birthday, was here feeling so inadequate. Like many other high school graduates, I'd been recruited, given a two-month summer course at Normal School, a temporary teaching certificate, and a copy of the curriculum, and was sent out to fill the gaps.

I didn't know how to fill out a register or make out required reports, what the prescribed texts were or how to get them, how to provide enough seatwork to keep little ones profitably occupied when I was busy with older grades, or how to make up a timetable that worked.

On the plus side, I had had several excellent teachers whose methods I would try to copy. I had taken Grades Nine and Ten by correspondence, so I knew what was involved in helping the five students who were taking those courses; Miss Wayland, the primary methods teacher at Normal, had given us a good grounding in teaching basic reading; I could play the piano and sing; and I knew how to play softball. As a bonus, I was tall, which proved to be important because several of the students were nearly as old as I, and even bigger. I had also inherited from my schoolteacher mother a wide interest in just about everything and a formidable tight-lipped glare that I could use if things started to get out of hand.

While I was mulling this over and trying to decide how I would fill the day, the children arrived. I rang the bell at nine, and about twenty youngsters took their seats. I wrote my name on the blackboard and said, "Class, stand." I knew it was customary to sing "O Canada," but for some reason what came out of my mouth was "We will sing 'God Save the King,'" so we did. I managed to remember the words to the Lord's Prayer and then took out the register, messing up the pronunciation of a couple of Romanian names and sending snickers through my audience. They had had a substitute teacher during August, so I spent the next few hours figuring out how far everyone had progressed in math and literature.

After lunch and a story chapter, I decided to follow the advice of Mr. Murray, our Normal School science teacher, which was to involve the whole class in learning something new about something they were familiar with. I had everyone go outside and catch grasshoppers. When each student held a specimen, and I did too, I helped them to find ears on the knee joints, breathing spiracles on the abdomen, two sets of wings, two compound and three simple eyes, and other peculiarities of insect construction. Everyone seemed interested, although there was a bit of commotion down in the Grade One area. Two little boys got tired of holding their hoppers so they pulled the hind legs off of them. Unable to hop, they just walked around on top of the desks. I gave a little talk on not being cruel to animals, quickly killed the maimed hoppers, and we released the rest into the schoolyard as a thank you for their help.

Three-thirty finally came. We sang "O Canada." I dismissed the class, corrected the exercise books that had been handed in, and prepared the next day's assignments. I also prepared about four times as much seat work for the beginners as I had ready for the first day. Those little fellows sure went through it fast.

I walked home, tired and feeling like a failure. You can imagine my relief when my landlady, who was mother of three of my students, told me that her kids had asked if it really was my first school, because I seemed to know what I was doing. It occurred to me that maybe my real calling should have been as an actress.

THE OLD RED GRANARY

A relic that still
comes in handy

On any trip around the prairies, the observer will notice rows of silver or white, round grain bins with dunce-cap roofs in every farmyard. Some, the hopper-bottoms, stand on stilts; they are the elite among bins, because although they do not hold as many bushels of grain, they funnel the grain out the bottom, rather than having to be shovelled out clean. The number of bins is a barometer of the size of the farm.

When I was a kid, a big farm might be three quarter-sections, less than one-tenth of a large farm today. Grain was stored undercover in many odd places in emergencies— once in a while even in a spare room in the house—but every farmer wanted to have two or three bright red wooden granaries, each twelve by sixteen feet, ten feet high, with a peaked roof, a small opening in the back peak for the grain spout of the threshing machine, and a bigger, front door that was planked up as the bin filled. Heavy skids under the floor allowed the bin to be moved to whatever field was being threshed.

The main accessory was a grain shovel, not the light aluminium ones we use today, but heavy, black, steel shovels that were used to fill the far corners of the bins and to keep the grain away from the unloading spout. When we were little, Carolie and I loved to play in the wheat. She has a cute dimple in her cheek, the result of playing too close behind the shoveller. We weren't so keen, though, on doing the "corner-filling" when we grew big enough to be useful, or on helping load wagon boxes backed up to the granary door when it came time to haul grain to town. Then, we would have to shovel the grain *out* of the far corners, panting and sweating and envying Dad's skill as he threw his shovelfuls out into the wagon box, exactly where he wanted them, with a smooth, strong rhythm.

An empty granary was versatile. It might provide a private bedroom for the hired man, where he could retire in comfortable squalor and smoke to his heart's content. It could be a playhouse for us girls, where we alternated amongst making mud pies, sieving sand, and collecting derelict bird nests, pretty rocks, and other messy treasures. Once in a while we became feverish housekeepers, sweeping and tidying in anticipation of a visit from Mrs. Brown. Mrs. Brown was a chatty visitor who enjoyed pretend coffee and cookies. She bore a startling resemblance to our mother.

With the end of summer came clean-up time. Our possessions were evicted, and we had to leave the floor clean. Dad had an irritating habit: when he came to inspect what we thought was a good job, he would bang the walls, bringing down all the grain kernels that had hidden in the cracks, and then we had to sweep the floor again.

In winter an empty granary was partitioned into bins for chop and oats, the farm animals' winter supplements. After freeze-up, cured hams, slabs of bacon, and frozen chunks of meat from the early winter butchering were buried in the oat bin, where they were protected from sudden thaws.

As these useful buildings became old and grey, they were given first aid: old licence plates and tin can lids were tacked over mouse holes; twisted wire ropes that connected fencepost braces on the outside walls interlaced each other to keep the old walls from collapsing outward with the weight of the grain; oil cans with bottoms and tops removed were split, flattened, and used to replace missing shingles.

❖

The Kopperud barn, granaries, wagon, and binder—
relics of the days when we farmed with horses

When they were finally replaced by sleek, sturdy, steel bins, these relics weren't necessarily abandoned. Sometimes they were tucked away in the corner of the yard, where they became repositories for old tires that might come in handy for the grain loader, leaky garden hoses that just need a couple of connectors to make them usable, good-as-new binder canvases that don't fit the big swather, chunks of iron rod that might be needed, rototillers that don't roto any more, and a couple of sets of harnesses that bring back too many memories to discard.

Now I appreciate big, efficient machinery, and my back and arms do not resent the grain loader and bin sweeps that make our work easier. But, like the old harnesses, the little granaries are an echo of days when neighbours were only a short walk away, parents and children worked and played alongside each other, and nobody threw anything away. I kind of hope the little old grey bins in the corner of the yard last as long as I do.

THE COOK CAR

*In praise of a little diner
and the women who kept
the harvest wheels rolling*

Sixty years ago, when I was a child, the day of the cook car had nearly ended. We kids were fortunate, though, because Dad had one that was parked just outside the trees. It had been used in the steam-engine days before he and Grandpa got a gas-fuelled tractor and a threshing machine, and it still contained some of the original equipment. We girls thought it would make a dandy playhouse, but the grownups were all for keeping it as it was, ready to go in case they might need it, someday.

A cook car was the forerunner of the travel trailer. A long, narrow room with a shed roof, with several small four-pane windows on each side, it was mounted on a wagon-like chassis. Steel-spoked wheels with flat, wide metal tires were under each corner, connected with axles to a wooden reach. On one end, a pole and doubletree enabled a team of horses to pull it; on the other end were a door and a set of removable steps.

Just inside the door were two narrow trestle tables flanked with wooden benches. Each table could accommodate four men per side at a setting. Near the far end, at the "front" of the cook car, sat a cookstove. Behind the stove, a narrow compartment held the cooks' bed, above which their clothing hung on nails. A flimsy curtain, strung across in front of the bed, gave the illusion of privacy.

The larger half of this end, in front of the stove, was the cook's workshop. Wooden shelves held enamel plates, deeply dished, plus enamel mugs that each accommodated about two cupfuls, with metal handles that became as hot as the coffee itself. A box held cutlery, a set of inexpensive, unadorned stamped steel, supplemented by odds and ends from the house or picked up at auction sales. Canned goods and bags of raisins and coffee joined the cream jug, sugar bowl, large serving bowls, salt and peppers, and big, white enamel milk jugs on the shelves.

On hooks beneath hung an enormous bread-mixing pan, its lid, three or four heavy, black frying pans, dishpans, a potato pot, saucepans, a roaster, and black metal bread pans. On top of the stove's warming oven half a dozen tin pie pans, a drippings container, and the salt can kept the alarm clock company. The coffee pot and tea kettle sat on the stove, ready for action. The coffee pot was enamel-ware, flat and wide at the bottom, tapering up to the top where a spout had been fastened over little holes that supposedly strained the brew. Its tin lid with a metal knob, the loop handle opposite the spout, and the wire bail handle all became as hot as the contents. It took finesse and strength to pour coffee—many were the spills and scalds.

Along the wall facing the stove, the worktable held a water crock, complete with dipper, hand basin, and soap dish. Hand towels were hung on a nail and the dishtowels on a line strung over the stove. Under the worktable was room for sacks of potatoes, beans, and onions, maybe some jars of pickles and canned vegetables, the sugar bin, and the lard and butter crocks. A flour bin at one end of the table and a wood box beside the stove completed the very functional workplace, but with the stove fired up non-stop in the hot days of harvest, and only a low roof, imagine the heat and stress of working there. The cooks, usually a mature woman and a girl to help her, worked as hard, and longer than, the harvesters.

Outside the cook car, on the shady side, a box with shelves and cloth-covered doors kept prepared food, sides of bacon, and fresh meat slightly cooler than they would have been indoors. A rickety wooden bench with soap and a couple of wash basins sat beside a water barrel. A few towels and a heavy comb tied to a long string hung from nails to complete the amenities. It was not considered good form to sit down to eat without tidying up a bit, and any man who didn't was soon clued in by his fellow diners.

The head cook's job was to keep the stove hot, bake bread, cakes, and pies, roast or fry the meat, make coffee, and generally make sure everything was ready to eat at mealtime. The helper brought in wood and water, prepared vegetables, washed dishes and towels, laid tables, cleared them, and did whatever else the cook asked her to, meanwhile learning enough so that someday she could be head cook and boss someone else around.

Breakfast at six in the morning was porridge, bacon, eggs, fried potatoes, bread with butter and jam, and coffee. Instant oatmeal didn't exist back then, so the porridge had been partly cooked the evening before. Bread sponge was also set to rise in the evening after the dishes were done.

Dinner (the noon meal) and supper were hearty meals: meat, potatoes, gravy, vegetables, pickles, and bread, with pie for dessert. The mid-afternoon lunch, usually sandwiches, cake, and coffee, was prepared and taken to the men in the field. Meals didn't take long to eat. There was little conversation. Everyone was intent on filling himself quickly so he could spend the rest of the hour (allowed mainly to give the horses time to eat and rest) finding a bit of shade and having a smoke. Smoking wasn't permitted near the threshing rig and was frowned upon in the field, where there was so much dry straw. Fire was a constant threat.

When the gas tractor replaced the cumbersome steam engine as power for the threshing machine, the crew became smaller. Men who had hauled water and straw to fuel the steam engine were no longer needed. It was now more convenient to move the machinery to where granaries were set up, so the men who had hauled grain in wagons and shovelled it off into bins were not required. Long hauls with sheaf-loaded racks from distant fields were replaced by frequent moves and shorter hauls, so fewer rack men were hired. Eight or ten men now accomplished what two dozen used to do. The days of the cook car were over.

As for the women, their job did not get easier, only now they didn't get paid for it. When the threshers arrived, a farm woman was expected to prepare a feast for ten extra men for three or four days in her usually small home, with none of the conveniences enjoyed by a professional cook-car cook. She spent the week before stocking up on baking and the week afterward trying to recover. Threshing went by in a hurried daze, with much anxious looking at the sky and praying that there would be no rain to prolong the threshers' stay. We daughters ended up being the cook's helpers, but because it was a break from the routine of school, and taking lunch out to the field was pretty exciting, we looked forward to it. The farm women often helped each other out, especially at dinnertime, coming early enough to help peel vegetables and set the table, and staying until the dishes were done and lunch was well under way. It was a stressful time, but with prairie co-operation and a lot of spunk, we always looked forward to harvest and back on it with fond memories.

Cook cars and their contents didn't evaporate. Some were taken to a lake, where they were divested of their wheels to become cabins, some were used as chicken coops or brooder houses, and some were taken apart and the wood used in other projects. Ours became part of a lean-to bedroom Dad added to the house as the family enlarged. The coffee pots usually went to a local hall and years later were still in service for midnight lunch. They became collectors' items. When some no-good vandals stole the local hall piano, they took the coffee pots as well. It is my sincere hope that, before they sold them, they tried them out and scalded themselves severely.

KIDS AND MONEY

We sold frogs and picked nails,
and it didn't hurt us a bit

Late in the fall, sixty-some years ago, when the folks made their annual trip to Swift Current to stock up on underwear, overshoes, and such at Cooper's department store, Carolie and I were each given a quarter and left on the opposite side of the street at Woolworth's five-and-dime. Pondering our purchases kept us safe and occupied for hours. We had to choose from little celluloid dolls with movable arms, a roll of crepe paper to make angel costumes for them, barrettes, all-nickel investments, or perhaps, throwing caution to the winds, a card of bobby pins or curlers, a genuine glass diamond ring, a fancy comb, or Lily of the Valley perfume, each of which cost a dime. We knew the value of money, because that was about the only time we didn't have to work for it.

Not that we were always paid for work. Chores like tending the farm animals, picking peas, weeding, dishwashing, dusting, and making beds were not paid jobs. I guess they were considered our contribution to the family's welfare. The days of allowances had not yet arrived.

Saturday afternoons often found us girls scouring the yard and driving lanes for nails and broken glass that might ruin tires. Dad paid us a cent for each five items. We usually quit at a nickel's worth, enough for an ice cream cone, or else three liquorice pipes and two suckers when we, like

Cousins Virginia and LaVerne perch in front of Grandpa Kopperud's house, 1927.

the rest of the local farmers, went to Cadillac for the weekly shopping trip. We also received a cent for every gopher we snared in the pasture and fields, but that was more fun than work. Getting first, second, or third ribbons in school field meets was often accompanied by a chit that could be turned in at the booth for candy or ice cream. Seeing as there were often no more than two or three kids of the right age in each event, the odds were pretty good that we would earn something.

Our best opportunity came during our summer holiday week at Lac Pelletier. We offered to run errands (and often were just thanked, not paid) and scavenged empty pop bottles to be redeemed at the snack booth. One year, some old Norwegian bachelors who spent hours rowing and fishing out in the middle of the lake offered us a quarter each for small frogs to use as bait. That was a bonanza. We really cashed in. Mother thought we shouldn't take the money, as they were neighbours, but Dad said, "Let them take it. Those guys will only spend it on drink anyway."

That summer, Mr. McIntyre, the man from Swift Current who made the mechanical horse "Dynamite" that was featured in every July 1st parade down Centre Street for decades, brought a merry-go-round to Lac Pelletier. We spent some of our frog loot riding it at ten cents for a five-minute whirl. When we ran out of money, Mr. McIntyre let us ride for free if we sang. No problem. We sang everything we knew and then started over. He thought it was good for business, as people stopped to listen and were enticed to ride. Years later I discovered the meaning of "shill." I guess that's what we were.

I don't know if kids who collect a regular allowance are that much luckier than we were. Nothing makes a kid, or an adult for that matter, appreciate the value of a dollar like having to put a bit of sweat into earning it.

ALL DOCTORED UP

The war against the common cold started a long time ago

We kids didn't get sick much, back in the Thirties when I was growing up. For one thing, it didn't pay. I faked a stomach ache one morning when I particularly didn't feel like going to school. Mother sympathized briefly, felt my forehead, and sent me back to bed. She assured me that, seeing as I was sick, I wouldn't feel like reading or playing, so she pulled down the blinds and left me to stew in my own juice. I recovered in time to go to school that afternoon.

Of course, nearly every winter some disease or other would be picked up at school. One at a time, we would come down with German measles or chickenpox or one of the other illnesses that was spotty or itchy or made us cough. Mom would consult the old doctor book to decide what this batch of symptoms meant. She would then resign herself to several weeks of nursing—or months if we didn't all get sick at the same time.

There wasn't much to be done about measles or mumps, except to endure them. When it came to colds, though, we were thoroughly "doctored up." When a sniffle turned into a cold, our parents went to war. Vicks VapoRub, one of the few patent medicines that we used, was rubbed on our necks and chests and upper lips, scratchy woollen socks were pinned around our necks, and we were plumped into bed under a couple of quilts to "sweat it out."

If that didn't work, Mom and Dad brought out the big guns. This consisted of a hot mustard foot bath on the bottom end, while we sat with the top end draped in towels and breathing in steam flavoured with Vicks or Friars' Balsam over bowls of boiling water. When the steam died down, we dried our feet and our red faces and submitted to having our chests, backs, and necks rubbed with a mixture of goose grease and turpentine. This was covered with an itchy wool wrap around our necks and down our chest and back. Meanwhile, Dad fixed us each a hot toddy: a little spoonful of brandy mixed with sugar and half a glass of very hot water (this was the only good part of the treatment). Then back to sweat under the quilts.

Occasionally Mom would give us each a quinine tablet. I don't think she knew what good they did, but she had bought them at the Rexall "one-cent sale," and the label stated, "For colds and fever," and the dosage for children, so we got it.

And if all that didn't work, Mom and Dad had several more arrows for their bows. A mustard plaster, a mix of one part powdered mustard, four parts flour, and enough water to make a paste, was spread on brown wrapping paper, the cold, wet result stuck on a bare chest or back, and left for twenty minutes. By the end of that time, your chest was on fire and the germs should have been burned up. Whatever the logic involved, it usually worked. Mother made her first-ever mustard plaster from mustard and water alone, with no flour to bate it, resulting in a nice batch of blisters. I'm glad she learned the proper mix before she had to treat us kids.

A croupy cough brought out the steam tent. Sheets were draped over the head of the bed to enclose us, and a little lamp with a pot on top was brought into play. The pot held a magenta-coloured oil that vapourized (it smelled awful) when the lamp was lit. This procedure was carefully monitored because of the danger of fire.

When I get together with my brothers and sisters these days, we often reminisce and smile at the memory of all the old "doctoring up" we endured. We treat our children and grandchildren with cold capsules, nasal sprays, and all the remedies available on the shelves of the modern drugstore. But Mom and Dad brought five kids safely through to adulthood, and we can claim nothing more.

THE DOCTOR BOOK

A book as important as the Bible and the Eaton's catalogue

I notice on the television ads that the "doctor book" is making a comeback. What this says about our health-care system is hard to evaluate, but I can predict safely that modern doctor books will never loom as large in life as the one I remember from my childhood.

When we kids broke out in spots or rashes, the folks would get us to stand near while they paged through the "Doctor Book." Then they would look at our spots, poke them to see if they came back with a red bit in the middle, or have us cough while they tried to decide whether hoarse, raspy, or wheezy was the apt description. They checked for rashes on the chest, behind the knees, or on the forehead. They decided for or against fevers, red eyes, black dots inside the cheek, and other miscellaneous effects until they had sorted out enough symptoms to decide if what we had was German measles or chickenpox or whatever. Then they checked the fine print to find out how long we had to stay home from school, sighed, and put the book away.

The Doctor Book was stored on a high shelf next to the family Bible, but not for the same reason. It was not considered fit literature for children. Of course, that only made it more intriguing. I managed to get hold of it quite a few times, usually on the sly. My parents never really censored what we read, but sneaking the Doctor Book from off the shelf and keeping one ear open for grownups added to the fascination.

The Doctor Book even looked like a serious book. It had a black cover with an engraved gold title and was about three inches thick. The end papers were swirls of mottled blue, dull green, and pale yellow with little red streaks here and there. I used to think that is what people's insides would look like—mottled blue, green, and yellow with little red blood vessels. I have since seen bits and pieces of the TV show *The Operation* and find that my vision was not that far from the truth.

There were two colour sections. One showed pestilences, plagues, and grisly conditions in nauseating, gory detail, from blotchy faces to swollen limbs, and from gangrenous toes to leprosy. I didn't spend much time on those pages.

The other colour section was probably what made the book taboo to children. It contained a series of transparencies. The top page showed a man clad only in his skin. It was like undressing a paper doll, because when that page was lifted, the next one showed all his muscles. Little blue lines connected each muscle to its scientific name. Lift the muscle page and it was like opening the hood of a car: the liver, heart, kidneys, brain, and all the rest of the machinery were laid out in full colour. The bare eyes—gruesome orbs staring out at me with no lids or lashes—were far more spectacular or riveting than any of the bits that might have concerned the grownups.

I more or less leafed through the rest of the book. The print was small and the words long and hard to understand. There were lots of recipes. None of them seemed very appetizing. They seemed to include a lot of things like powdered sulphur, oily stuff, and Epsom salts.

The Doctor Book was a far cry from the health services we take for granted these days and was probably out of date even in the 1930s. However, it helped Mom and Dad cure ringworm, soothe the pain of an earache, ease the irritation of chickenpox or nettlerash, deal with boils, cuts, bruises, and sprains, and rule out such disasters as scurvy or tapeworms. The book wasn't infallible, but when it was the only help available for a crying child on a long winter night, I'm sure they felt it deserved its honoured position, up on the high shelf, next to the Bible.

HOME REMEDIES

Home remedies that
worked—more or less

When I was a child, the drugstore in Cadillac was a little square building on Main Street. Dr. Porter, who owned it, had his office in the back. Shelves of bottles and metal containers lined one wall, and a glass-fronted display case on the other side held Parker's fountain pens, cosmetics in fancy containers, and gift-boxed razors, dresser sets, shaving mirrors, and other presents for momentous occasions. The oiled floor and wainscoted walls emphasized that this was a serious establishment, where nothing as frivolous as a soda fountain would be appropriate.

Nowadays, drugstores are huge, bright superthings selling everything from Hallowe'en masks to salad dressing. One aisle is devoted to cosmetic aids and another to dozens of brands of patent medications for the "cure-it-myself" crowd. How did people ever get along without such convenience?

My parents and grandparents were pioneers, both in Saskatchewan and in Minnesota. Except for emergencies such as appendicitis, broken bones, and disastrous epidemics like typhoid and diphtheria, they never saw a doctor. They relied on folk medicine.

I am just old enough to remember being treated with some of those remedies, and others I heard about from my dad. I remember plunging my frostbitten feet and hands into buckets of cold water to relieve the agony as they "thawed out." It was blessed relief. Dad's big toes froze nearly every winter in spite of the felt boots he wore. He kept a jar of pig gall to rub on them to relieve the pain.

I cut my ankle on a roll of barbed wire when I tried to jump out of the fencing wagon, where I wasn't supposed to be in the first place. In a couple of days a little red line started to creep up my swollen leg. BLOOD POISON! A handful of Epsom salts was sprinkled into a pail of hot water—very hot water as I remember it—and I had to soak my foot and leg every two hours. It must have helped because I still have my leg, and the scar on my ankle, too.

A chest cold called for a rubbed-in mixture of turpentine and goose grease. Dad said turpentine and skunk oil worked better, but either we were short of skunks, or short of anybody willing to de-oil one, because we never had that mix. If pneumonia or pleurisy threatened, a mustard plaster was required, but it easily caused blisters and so was reserved for do-or-die cases.

I had an earache when I stayed overnight at Grandma Kopperud's. She heated olive oil in a teaspoon, held it to her lip to test the temperature, poured it into my ear, and stuffed cotton batting on top of it. Then she heated a small cotton bag full of salt in the oven. That went between my ear and the pillow, and I went to sleep.

Butter also figured as a remedy. A modern first aider would have a fit if anyone tried to soothe burns and scalds with sweet (unsalted) butter nowadays, but that was how they did it sixty years ago. A ringworm infection was cured with burnt butter. I asked a doctor about that once, and after hemming and hawing a bit, he said that salicylic acid is used in present-day remedies and that the butyric acid in burnt butter would probably be effective, too.

A paste of baking soda and water was used to relieve the itch of mosquito bites and was also used to soothe burns. A handful of baking soda in the bath water eased the discomfort of sunburn as well as chickenpox. It also got into the cosmetic area, because it was used for brushing teeth when we ran out of toothpaste, not without a lot of protest from us kids. I can still remember the taste!

I never experienced one of the plagues that my aunts and uncles remembered without fondness. Overcrowded schools and lack of sanitation sometimes led to epidemics of head lice. Male sufferers were cured by the drastic method of shaving the entire head. Females, proud of their long hair, preferred the kerosene treatment. The entire scalp and hair were soaked in kerosene and wrapped in towels for hours. This killed the active little fellows and softened the glue that fastened the nits, or eggs, to the base of the hairs. The nits were then picked out with a fine-tooth comb. (Yes, that is where the expression comes from.)

Grandma knew well that harvest crews were bound to carry body lice. When her sons and a daughter came home from a stint of threshing and cooking for harvesters, she set fresh clothing and two tubs of soapy water out in the trees. Each had to put all used clothing into one tub, bathe in the other, and don a fresh outfit before being allowed into the house.

Nobody ever owned up to having scabies, a mite that burrowed under the skin in the hidden hairy areas of the body, but even if nobody ever had it, it was cured with a mixture of sulphur and lard.

A couple of gruesome treatments I heard about but cannot vouch for are for thrush, a fungus infection in babies' mouths, and another remedy for blood poisoning. Thrush was supposedly cured by making the baby suck on a little live frog! I suppose someone had to hold the frog's legs so that the poor fellow didn't become a source of protein instead of a treatment. Is it possible that the slime on the frog's skin was anti-fungal? A soak in stale urine, usually available from the chamber pot under the bed, supposedly remedied blood poison. Maybe the ammonia or the solutes had some medicinal effect. Folk medicine usually worked, even if the practitioners didn't have any idea why.

Modern antibiotics may be produced by moulds or have some other disagreeable origin. Goodness knows, nobody thinks about the source of birth control pills when they are using them. It really doesn't matter these days because by the time the cure reaches the treatment area we haven't the faintest notion what we are using, and I, for one, like it that way.

OLD TOYS

*Why our playthings
never became antiques*

I have just come home from the gun, craft, and antique show in Saskatoon. Aside from an acute case of stiffness, brought on by four hours of ambling around on a concrete floor and a 350-mile round trip in the van, my main disorder is an acute case of chagrin. This is partly due to seeing so many household things, such as the eggbeaters, orange squeezers, and square, coloured Pyrex bowls that I once used, broke, and discarded, now all polished up and called antiques. Their price tags would more than pay for their electric and plastic successors. If I were a better fortune-teller, I would go through my kitchen and carefully pack away several boxes of future antiques, to support me in my *real* old age!

The rest of the chagrin comes from seeing the toys and games that are now collectibles. Oh, my children! You never realized how valuable your G-I Joes, Barbies, Dinky Toys, and wind-up trains were! Worse yet, neither did I!

I didn't recognize many toys from my own childhood. For one thing, we didn't have many toys, and those we did have were so well used that they would be valuable only in their owner's eyes. Anything that survived intact was passed on to younger siblings, until it too was but a shadow. I remember Carl and Kay playing cops and robbers, each armed to the teeth with one-half of a disintegrated cap gun. In some ways, it was an improvement over the original. They never ran out of yelling "Bang!" as they would have run out of caps, and they didn't have to bother threading those pesky little strips through the levers that lifted them under the hammer with each pull of the trigger.

I never saw my mother and father play tennis, but they had two old tennis racquets and a mangy tennis ball that served us kids well. Dad put up the old net, but we thought it was a lot more fun to play "Old Cat," a game played with a bat and baseball. What magnificent fly balls and sizzling grounders we could hit with the old racquets. The tennis ball not only improved our fielding ability, it was also a lot more bearable than a baseball if we caught it in the face or on the shins, instead of in our gloveless hands.

Every once in a while the tennis ball would end up in the bushes and would disappear forever, or at least until the leaves fell off. Until our sophisticated cousins, who played real tennis, donated another old ball to us, we were reduced to playing with a real hardball, one that was too dilapidated for the men's team to use. The tennis racquets couldn't handle the heavy hardball, so we made do with any approximation of a bat. I wonder if Carl still has that scar under his eyebrow. We found the broken handle of a pitchfork that had been wired together but broke again, so we decided to use the stub as a bat. Carl was the catcher, and the piece of wire clinging to the broken end nicked him just over the eye. Oh, my, he bled!

Carl also had the distinction of being harnessed to the little wagon and driven by his older sister (not me!). The harness was mostly binder twine and haywire, but they did have a real bit to put in his mouth. Of course, he couldn't talk around it, but he could prance and buck and neigh to his heart's content.

We each had a pair of skis, which were shapeless except for the bent-up toe, and the bindings consisted of straps into which we tucked the toes of our overshoes. With a tree branch or, if we were lucky, a piece of broken bamboo binder whip for a pole, we headed for Grandpa's pasture to meet our cousins. The cousins usually spent part of the long winter holidays with our grandparents, just the other side of the pasture. We climbed Grandpa's hill, slid down, fell off, and repeated that routine until we were too cold, wet, and tired to do more than creep home.

Our belly-flopper sleds had low, sharp runners, meant more for icy streets than big drifts, so they were used only by tying them behind the bobsleigh. We would cling to them, bouncing in and out of the sleigh ruts and horse tracks. If we fell off or let go, our patient dad would stop the horses and wait for us to run up and flop back down onto the sleds, hopefully with a better grip this time.

When it was too cold or stormy to frolic outside, Carolie and I played "Paper People" on the kitchen table. Although we reluctantly packed everything up for mealtimes, this game continued all winter. Our houses were corrugated cardboard cartons, laid on their sides. We cut windows and door holes in the downstairs and laid out the rooms. The top surface was the upstairs, which included bedrooms and a bath (a trifle airy with no walls except in our imagination). We usually had an imaginary staircase, too, as it was too hard to get corrugated cardboard to bend like steps but stay rigid enough to work well.

Our people were cut from a catalogue. They often had only one complete leg and a sliver of the second, because the catalogue makers were very inconsiderate in their placement of prices and descriptions. Our people were cut out and immediately bent at the waist and knees so they could sit on the chairs. This meant that they walked with an arthritic posture and slept with their legs waving in the air, but that didn't bother us at all.

The furniture was cut out of thinner cardboard and bent to shape. Chairs, beds, and chesterfields were easy to make. A sturdy table was a lot more difficult, as was a stove or icebox with doors that opened. The bath-tub was the inner box from Eddy's matches. Its slip-on cover, with flaps cut and bent up to make seats, was the car.

Carolie and I were the "giants" who made the house and furniture, moved the people, and provided the plot and dialogue. I was much more interested in making the furniture or trying to upholster it with cloth and flour paste, than in my people. My family was Mother, Father, and two children, and they mostly sat around on the furniture. Carolie's family was Mother, Father, about seven variously sized children, and two or three babies! They were all busily interactive and chatty.

Carolie loved visiting and would load the whole works into her matchbox car to come to visit my family. If Giant Me was busy creating, I would pop my people inside the house and bustle the father around all the doors and windows, saying, "Lock, Lock, Lock," and then put them all to bed. Her family would sit outside my box, frustrated. Even at our age now, she occasionally chides me for having been so miserable to her. (She still loves visiting and I have become much more hospitable.)

Our home was small, and I often wonder that Mother was so tolerant of the mess we made. She called it "clean dirt" and that phrase often comes to my mind when I walk around and over the paper, cardboard, scissors, and glue on the floor, because when my little grandsons visit, I get them playing Paper People, with cardboard cartons, the catalogue, and Corn Flakes boxes.

It is obvious why our toys will never grace the antique tables. I can't help feeling a bit sorry for the children who once owned the toys and games that are now collectibles. It seems to me that they couldn't have had much fun with them.

THE CHRISTMAS CONCERT

The night when every child was a star

Why was the Christmas concert such a big deal, anyway? Seniors and some not so senior get a faraway look in their eyes and a half-smile on their faces just remembering. In these days of slick programming on television and film, music at the turn of a knob, or even without, as in elevators and department stores, and videos on demand, it does seem a bit irrational for us to place so much value on the memory of what was surely a very amateur production. Well, let me take you back to a country school on the day of the Christmas concert.

The morning was hectic. The dress rehearsal, when all costumes and props were used, was a disaster. The whole class—and the teacher—were so keyed up that everything went wrong. Speeches, long memorized, were stumbled over; someone fell off the stage in the Star Drill; there weren't enough pins to fasten the crepe-paper costumes; the school organ had developed a wheeze. As she dismissed the class at noon with a smile, the teacher assured everyone that a bad rehearsal meant a good performance. In her heart she prayed that it was true, as she knew that her professional reputation could be made or broken by the concert, irrational as that seemed.

Shortly after six o'clock, teams of horses started to make their way through the snowdrifts toward the school.

White gas-lantern light beamed through the windows to welcome them. The rigs disgorged their cargo of mothers, babies, aunts, grandparents, and of course the schoolchildren—girls scarcely recognizable in their curls and ruffles, boys uncomfortable in their Sunday suits and fresh haircuts. The school room was transformed, too, with the desks arranged along the walls, plank benches in the centre, in one corner a magnificent green tree—all sparkly with ornaments, and the foot-high stage hidden from view by curtains, which, in their other lives, were white bedsheets. The children disappeared behind the curtains and sounded very busy and excited. On the seats the audience was just as noisy, as neighbours exchanged greetings, news, and compliments of the season.

The organ, its wheezing forgotten, began "O Canada," and the curtains opened to reveal all sixteen scholars standing at attention. The audience rose and everybody sang. The children, their nerves in tight rein, accompanied the noise of reseating with a rousing chorus of "We Wish You a Merry Christmas." The curtains closed and the chairman of the school board, in *his* Sunday suit and fresh haircut, welcomed his neighbours and, after clearing his throat several times, said he hoped they would all enjoy themselves and appreciate the work done to entertain them. Then he quickly sat down.

The curtains reopened to reveal three preschoolers lined up to recite verses. One little girl dissolved into tears and whispered her verse back to her mother, who was whispering it to her. The next girl, a budding extrovert, made a quick bow, shouted four lines about not intending to go to sleep on Christmas Eve, gave another quick nod, and smiled smugly. During the previous items, the remaining tot had reduced the entire room to silent hysterics by vigorously scratching various parts of his anatomy, all the while keeping his hands in his pockets and his eyes on the top of the Christmas tree. His verse was met with the same hearty applause as the others, and the curtains closed again.

The programme progressed with several comedy skits. Homer, a twelve-year-old who had steadfastly refused to speak in anything but a monotone during rehearsals, suddenly became inspired and wowed the audience with his version of a henpecked husband. Everyone studiously ignored the prompter's whisper when Carol was so overcome with stage fright that she could hardly talk, and they smiled encouragement as she recovered her poise.

The boys' Clown Drill was enjoyed and no one knew just whether the mistakes and bumping were on purpose or not. The Star Drill, seven tiny girls and two tall thirteen-year-olds, went beautifully, the crepe-paper costumes stayed together, nobody lost her wand, and everyone ignored lumps that long underwear made under long, brown stockings, even if they did detract from the air of grace and light that the performance was supposed to evoke.

Among the musical numbers was a duet by two sisters. They avoided looking at their mother, who was silently mouthing every word, her expressive face reflecting each idea in the song. A man standing over by the door thoroughly enjoyed the mother's performance, and the girls had to keep their eyes off him, too, or they knew they would break up and disgrace themselves.

The last item on every programme was the Nativity. In front of a backdrop of the Bethlehem countryside, made by the class from cardboard and crepe paper and complete with a glowing star, the entire school stood or knelt in bathrobes, sheets, and striped towels to represent shepherds, kings, Mary, Joseph, and the angels. Four little Grade Ones and Twos in fleecy white underwear, pink ears, and pinned-on tails were the "flocks by night" that the shepherds watched. Suddenly serious, they all kept their eyes on a swaddled doll that lay on a pile of golden straw. Their clear voices softly repeated old carols that told of shepherds on the hillsides, wise men on a quest, angel choirs at midnight. At a sign from the head angel, the audience joined in singing the old favourite, "Silent Night." As the bass and tenor voices of fathers and uncles, and the altos and sopranos of mothers and grandmothers joined in harmony with the children, there were a few eyes that brimmed over and quite a few lumps in various throats.

After the children reclaimed their own clothing, the chairman announced that he had heard a rumour that a sleigh and some odd animals had been noticed coming in from the north, and in a few minutes a rather skinny-legged Santa with a bulgy front burst in the back door with a "HO, HO, HO!" The teacher heaved a sigh of relief because she couldn't smell liquor when Santa gave her a quick hug. She had memories of other concerts and near catastrophes. Santa distributed the parcels from under the tree, a small gift from the teacher for each pupil, and one from each family for her, always including several boxes of fancy stationery and a big bottle of sweet-pea cologne. There was one gift that the teacher looked at and, blushing a little, put away to open privately. Candy bags were pulled from Santa's gunny sack before he hoisted it back over his shoulder and departed, saying that he was expected at another school and had to hurry.

Coffee and lunch appeared and disappeared, children were rounded up and bundled up, and the men left to bring the teams to the door. Children, suddenly sleepy, and women carrying babies or helping the elderly down snowy steps, made their way outside. The gas lanterns were extinguished. Nothing remained but a clutter of paper, orange peelings, and discarded costumes, to be tidied up the next day. Nothing else, that is, except the memories engraved into the hearts of every one of us who was lucky enough to have been a part of the Christmas concert.

TRADITIONS

Christmas "discomfort" is a tradition at my house

Christmas cards try so hard to be traditional. One that I remember from when I was a child opened up to make a cut-out scene. The back panel showed a long, snowy slope dotted with perfect fir trees. On the next one, there was a lamp-lit cottage, the roof covered with big, puffy snow pillows. In the front panel, the cut-out father was dragging an immense Christmas tree in the direction of the cottage while his son trudged beside him, carrying home the axe. I am sure the axe came in handy when they got home, either to cut the tree in half or else to open up the cottage roof, because that big tree was never going to stand up in that little cottage. It did seem such a Christmasy thing, though, cutting down your own tree—really traditional.

Traditions change. One of our prairie traditions is the, well, not an argument, more like a very warm discussion about whether to buy a tree when the first truckloads hit the lots and there are so many to choose from, and then watch it become dry and bare outside before it's time to trim it, or whether to wait until just before we're ready to decorate, then try to find something both bushy and green amongst the remnants in the tree lot. Either way, we seem to reap a rugful of needles. It is the traditional woodsy smell of a real tree that keeps us from buying the permanently green plastic and wire things. That and the thought that, as well as untrim the tree by myself (I have great difficulty getting enthusiastic, or any other kind of help, for that job), I would have to dust it and find some place for storage.

Using real wax candles on the tree, with the threat of setting the whole thing on fire, was a tradition, too, but thank goodness not any more. For a while it was sort of a tradition at our house to try to find out which bulb to replace when one burned out, but now we have those twinkle lights. I even have one string that looks like candles—as long as they're in their box. Once they're on the tree, they hang upside down or tip sideways the minute my back is turned. I do miss the lead-foil "rain" that we used to drape, piece by piece, on the end of each branch. The twenty thousand or so strands in every modern box of plastic rain are a pain to put on, stretch out sideways to grab every passing pant leg, and are nearly impossible to get rid of.

We kids used to write traditional letters to Santa. Mom mailed them in the stove. She somehow thought that because Santa came down the chimney, his mail could be delivered in reverse. Mostly our letters just told him what excellent children we were—we weren't encouraged to ask for specific things. Now the tradition is for givers to ask recipients for a long list of gift ideas to choose from.

Traditional gifts have changed, too. Kids used to get sleds, tea sets, baby dolls, trains, and carpenter sets; ties were for dads and perfume for moms, while slippers and embroidered hankies were for grandpas and grandmas. Now kids' lists include such items as Tickle Me Elmo, Star Wars doodads, Transformers, computer games, and the junk that TV ads push, that look like so much fun and turn out just as disappointing as my carpenter set. I got that when I was about eight. The teeny hammer head wasn't big enough to bash in a thumbtack, and besides, the face was nearly round, the claws were too thick to pull out a nail, and the head kept falling off. The saw was about eight inches long and bent double on the down stroke. About the only things I sawed with it were a couple of laths and the edge of the kitchen chair I was using as a sawhorse.

Once upon a time, the only things that came in pieces

were Meccano sets, Tinkertoys, and jigsaw puzzles. A new Christmas Day tradition is for older males in the family to wish they were mechanical engineers as they help impatient youngsters do the "easy assembly" required before play can begin. My kids were little when toys like Fort Apache and Lego became popular. Fort Apache had about eighty inch-high plastic soldiers, horses, and Indians, as well as a fort that came apart more easily than it went together. Lego blocks come in sets of about 347. It is a fact of life that no one can ever find all the pieces after the box is breached. That is the origin of the traditional Christmas limp of sock-footed grownups.

When I was young, there were enough relatives who lived near—or at least within an hour's drive with horses—that Christmas week, after the traditional Christmas church service, was filled with visits to aunts and uncles where we spent non-eating hours skating on the slough, sledding, playing noisy games of crokinole or pick-up-sticks, and singing around the piano. Our children and their families are so spread out across the Prairies that part of their Christmas tradition has been to pack up and travel home for the holidays. We have added TV's "A Christmas Carol" and "It's a Wonderful Life," Scrabble, video games, and snowmobiling to our traditional Christmas delights.

About the only tradition that hasn't changed is the turkey and trimmings. For one day a year, we ignore grams of fat, junk food phobias, and calories. Plates are piled high with whipped-cream salad, mashed potatoes doused in gravy, big slabs of turkey with crisp, brown skin, veggies in melted butter, pickles, and cranberry sauce. When everybody is full, big wedges of mince pie or bowls of Christmas pudding swimming in brown-sugar sauce arrive on the table, and are eaten up, too. I remember asking for just a sliver of apple pie at Nan and Gramp's and getting a quarter of a pie, covered with ice cream. The last two bites stayed on my plate for quite a while, but I did it! A couple of years ago, my twelve-year-old grandson remarked after dinner, "One thing, you always leave Grandma's table feeling uncomfortable." He meant it as a compliment, and I took it as one. Uncomfortable after dinner is a Christmas tradition.

CHRISTMAS 1937

When the spirit of Christmas conquered the Depression

My sister and I had nearly worn out the Eaton's catalogue. It contained about twelve pages of toys, and one of the pages was glossy, showing in magnificent colour a host of dolls, from the little black one with two bumps on her composition head, where red and white ribbon bows were tied, to the elegant "Eaton's Beauty" that had real hair. Not only did she have real curls but also real lashes on eyes that shut when she was laid down. She wore a ruffled bonnet, lace-trimmed pantaloons, white socks, and black, shiny booties that could be taken off and put on again. And her dress! It was just like a princess's gown, with puffy sleeves and ruffles on the full, long skirt, ruffles that started at the waist and arched down around the hem. The problem was that she cost nearly twenty dollars, and we knew very well that she was out of the question. There had been no crop for several years and we were broke. But it didn't cost anything to dream.

About a week before Christmas, we learned that a Christmas tree was too expensive as well. We suggested cutting down one of the few, small evergreens that Grandpa had planted around his house. They were just about the right size, we thought. Instead, Dad brought in a bushy poplar that hadn't made it through the hot, dusty, rainless summer. He propped up the leafless thing in a pail of sand.

Mom pulled out the box of decorations. We strung popcorn and made garlands out of strips of coloured paper from magazines, glued into interlocking circles with flour paste. When these and the little glass balls were distributed all over the wee bush, we assured each other, "You can hardly tell it isn't a real tree, can you?"

About this time, a box arrived in the mail from "the coast," wherever that was. Our uncle and aunt had sent us little gifts and had filled the rest of the box with branches of holly, bright green and prickly, with a few bright red berries shining through. Mom saved a branch for each of the other relatives, and there was still enough left to decorate the windows and a sprig to put on the front door. The house looked beautiful!

Somehow Carolie and I had mislaid our best dolls, from last Christmas, but we were really too busy to play with dolls anyhow. Grandma had given us each a square of hemmed muslin, marked with a transfer pattern, and we were supposed to embroider handkerchiefs for our present to Mom. Grandma was pretty fussy about stuff like that, and we knew she would check the back of the embroidery to make sure we hadn't made ugly knots or long stitches. Dad was unusually busy in the basement, hammering and sawing, and we weren't allowed to go down there.

Between bouts at the sewing machine, Mom made carrot pudding, melt-in-your-mouth rosettes and fattigman, and a flat bread so thin and crisp that it was nearly impossible to butter and eat neatly, as well as *lefse*, a thin, potato-based bread that, when cut into triangles, buttered and rolled up, was just about the best food ever invented. Mom was famous for her mincemeat pies, although Carolie and I didn't much appreciate them. Our parents would take their turn during Christmas week, hosting all the relatives, and all this food had to be ready ahead of time.

There is one other kind of food for which Scandinavians are famous—or maybe infamous: *lutefisk*. Back in Norway, *lutefisk* and *lefse* were poor man's food. For *lutefisk*, codfish was soaked in a lye ("lute" in Norwegian) bath to kill all bacteria, and then would keep all winter long. To be

*The Kopperud cousins—Eileen, LaVerne, Carolie, Alvera,
Thora, Frayne, and Baby Carl, 1935*

used, it had to be soaked and rinsed many times to get rid of all the lye. Then the chunks were simmered until firm and nearly transparent, and eaten with boiled potatoes and melted butter. It is an acquired taste, and we children didn't much care for it. (I love it now and buy it every Christmas, already soaked, frozen, and ready to cook, although *my* children don't much care for it.)

During part of the 1930s, people from eastern Canada sent carloads of apples, cheddar cheese, and salted, dried cod to Saskatchewan, to be distributed as relief. The apples and cheese were universally welcomed, but the flat, salt-filled, whole fish were a real problem to many, and much of it was discarded. Not by the Norskies. They soaked the salt out with many rinses, treated it to a lye bath for several days, then soaked and rinsed the lye out, and what do you know—*lutefisk*! How much food value was left after all the soaking and rinsing is debatable, but it looked like *lutefisk* and tasted like *lutefisk*, and they loved it.

Christmas Eve finally arrived. Milking and other chores were done early. Dad gave each animal an extra bit of oat chop and then set a wheat sheaf upright on a post, Christmas for the birds. We all put on our best clothes and climbed into the horse-drawn cutter to drive the half-mile to Grandpa's house. Sometimes it must have been cloudy, but I always remember it with starlight on the white hills, squeaking bobsleigh runners on the crisp snow, the jingle of the harness, and a faint horsy smell from the blankets that covered us on the trip, and would cover the horses after we got there.

A burst of steam haloed Grandma as she opened the kitchen door to greet us. We quickly stacked our coats and leggings onto the growing pile on Grandma's bed and ran to play with our cousins. The uncles all sat around in the kitchen, watching the aunts stirring gravy and filling bowls with mashed potatoes, creamed peas and carrots, meatballs, *lutefisk*, and melted butter. In those days, the grownups ate at the first table, and they always seemed to take such a long time about it, but pretty soon the plates were washed and the table reset. We children ate with

Grandma and one or two of the younger aunts who had waited on the first table. We ate quickly, said our "takk for mat" (thanks for the meal) and "excuse me" to Grandma, then went to join the grownups around the piano in the living-room.

We sang all the old carols and some not so familiar ones in Norwegian. Dad and Uncle Oliver sang bass, Garry and Jul tenor, and some of the aunts could switch between soprano and alto. The volume was maybe more suited to a large hall than to the living-room, but it was glorious anyway. Then one of the cousins was asked to read the Christmas story from Luke. It didn't matter if "Cyrenius, governor of Syria" was mispronounced. Everyone knew it by heart, anyway.

When Grandma passed around a plate of oranges and candy, and Grandpa started peeling Brazil nuts with his pocket knife for the youngsters, we knew the climax was nearing. All of a sudden, there was a racket and banging from the veranda, and in came Santa, with his face muffled in a scarf, wearing Grandpa's buffalo coat and fur hat, and galoshes. He dragged in boxes of gifts and ruffled our hair and bearhugged anybody he could catch—even the aunts!

Carolie and I each got a little doll bed, complete with bedding, and a little wooden trunk. Inside the trunk was, not an Eaton's Beauty, for sure, but our misplaced dolls, each with a new outfit: a ruffled bonnet, wee socks, and a silky dress with puffy sleeves and ruffles that arched from the waistline all down around the hem, just like a princess.

There have been Christmases since with more extravagant gifts, more exotic food, and more elegant decorations, but I don't think the spirit of Christmas could be surpassed by the gifts of love, that depression year, when Mom turned rags and remnants into bedding and a princess dress, Dad made apple boxes into doll furniture, and the little dry bush was trimmed with glass balls, paper garlands, and strings of popcorn.

THE EATON'S
CATALOGUE

A "wish book" that was
appreciated down to the spine

Several times a year a postcard appears in our mailbox, urging me to stop in and pick up the new catalogue. The fall and winter one is ready about the time I am picking peas or swatting mosquitoes, and the spring and summer one usually comes when I am busy un-decorating the Christmas tree. Seven or eight sale editions arrive sporadically throughout the year. Catalogues aren't the big deal they used to be when I was a kid.

The Eaton's catalogue usually arrived in early fall and was good for the entire year. Most of the pages were printed black and white on unglazed paper, but ten or twelve pages were glossy, displaying the more expensive dresses, coats, hats, suits, and dolls in full, glorious colour. It was like having a city full of stores right in our own home.

The hardware "store" displayed tools such as hammers, saws, and clamps, as well as harnesses, black and shiny on chunky Clydesdale horses with fat, feathery feet. The ladders, paint and brushes, rakes, hoes, and slim garden cultivators made our old tools, with their haywire patches and slivery handles, look positively archaic.

The furniture "store" had bedroom suites with waterfall-top dressers, all matching. For an elegant look in the dining room, we could purchase a huge pedestal table with a buffet, a china cabinet, and six matching chairs—five ordinary ones and the "daddy" one with arms. The kitchen cabinets, each with a pull-out enamel work surface, were chock-full of little shelves and drawers and sifter flour bins. New ranges, big and black with shiny nickel trim all over the place, looked so easy to clean, and there were even some kerosene stoves with removable ovens for summer days when the house was too hot to bear using the wood stove. You could buy a child's high chair, complete with tray, for $2.25 or, if that stretched the pocket too much, forty-nine cents down and twenty-five cents a month for ten months!

There were the clothing store, the shoe store, the fabric store, and the china shop, and even a toy store—twelve whole pages of that.

I remember Mom and Dad sitting at the kitchen table, writing and revising their lists, mostly underwear, socks, and overalls, and drawing the outline of our feet on a piece of paper to get the right shoe sizes. Then they would add up the total and strike out a few things before copying the list onto the order form. The day the parcel arrived was nearly as exciting as Christmas.

The catalogue's usefulness didn't end there. The pages could be folded and moulded to make an umbrella-shaped doorstop. Colour pages could be cut into little pieces and glued to a bottle to make an attractive vase. Plain pages could be torn into tiny pieces and soaked in flour paste to make papier-mâché. We girls populated our paper-doll houses with families cut out of the catalogue. Boys were said to use it to discover the secrets of feminine undergarments. New Canadians who had been taught in other languages used it to learn to read English. It nourished the daydreams and aspirations of many of us in those hand-me-down, make-over, depression days.

And, of course, after the new catalogue arrived, we bored a hole into the top corner of the old one and hung it in the outdoor toilet. There the procedure was, after sitting down, to rip off a page and use the interim to squash, wrinkle, and rumple it. It took a while to get the shine off and make it usable. It also gave us something useful to do while waiting.

GOOSEBERRIES AND COMFORT FOOD

If it's white and doesn't need chewing, it has to be good for the soul

I picked the gooseberries this morning, not one of my favourite jobs. My arms are scored with scratches—not deep enough to bleed but they smart a bit, and I have several punctures in my fingers. Later on, I will sit in my big chair and remove the gooseberry tails and noses with my thumbnail, berry by berry. Sometime soon I will make gooseberry jam, a favourite in our house. Why all this fuss? Well, do you know that you can't buy gooseberry jam in stores anymore?

We eat out quite a bit these days, much more than we used to when the kids lived at home. For one thing it is easier to pay the tab for two than for five, and the kids now have the privilege of paying for their own shoes, sports, and special yearnings, so our "mad money" doesn't evaporate the way it used to. I enjoy choosing a meal without worrying about making it. I enjoy being waited on. Most of all I enjoy getting up and leaving the cleaning and dishes for somebody else to do. For people who were raised on things such as oatmeal porridge, or meat, potatoes and gravy, we have become really cosmopolitan. We take shrimp, burritos, pizza, or sweet and sour chicken balls as a matter of course. But like gooseberry jam, there are some things that can't be bought.

Bread pudding, for example. I do what Mom used to—

break three or four eggs into a casserole, add sugar, milk, nutmeg, salt, and vanilla, then beat everything to a froth. There isn't a recipe; I think measuring things for bread pudding is probably against the law. Then I break up four or five slices of dry bread into the custard and sprinkle a handful of raisins on top. Next I moosh it around a bit, put it in the oven for half an hour, and watch people come back for seconds and thirds. It is not on any menu.

Strawberry shortcake may be on the menu, but don't bother ordering it. All you get is a chunk of cake made from a mix, some white fuzzy stuff from an aerosol can sprayed on in professional swirls, and a couple of huge, vividly red but tasteless berries sliced up on top. Looks great and tastes like glue. I am sure there must be some chef in some eating place who knows that he should make large, rich baking powder biscuits, with a little extra sugar and shortening, split them when just out of the oven, slather butter and sugared, sliced berries on the bottom half, put the lid on, and cover the works with real whipped cream and whole berries. There must be such a chef, but I have never found him. Maybe the cholesterol police have put him away.

Mashed potatoes have disappeared. Remember that I grew up on them. These days potatoes are considered mashed if they are scrunched up a bit and left lumpy, grey, and wet. Real mashed potatoes are white and smooth, whipped with milk and margarine so that they stand proudly peaked on the plate. Mixed steamed vegetables are sort of iffy. I have nothing against raw crisp *cold* vegetables, but I think that steamed vegetables should be exposed to steam for longer than fifteen seconds. I expect to be able to insert a fork into a sprig of steamed broccoli without undue exertion, and I expect it to be hot. And whatever happened to sticky, gooey rice like Mother used to make? I am not keen on fighting with fluffy rice, each kernel pristinely white and independently averse to staying on a fork for the twelve-inch trip from the plate to my mouth.

Something that is rarely seen on menus is "comfort

food." According to psychologists and folklore, comfort food is white, semi-solid, and doesn't need to be chewed. We need comfort food when it is stormy, or when romance has gone sour, or when your head aches and your nose runs and nobody seems to care. When I am blue or out of sorts, I make milk soup—just dumplings cooked in hot milk. I think it is a dish Mom invented to fill our stomachs during the hard times when what we ate was only what the farm provided. Or else I make myself "cream and bread"—a slice of white bread soaked in cream and sprinkled with brown sugar. Now I can't buy stuff like that—but, of course, if it is nice enough outside and I am perky enough to go out to eat, I really don't need comfort food, do I?

FUEL FOR THOUGHT

Why I am happy
to pay the fuel bill

About the middle of every month, a big fuel truck rolls into our farmyard, feeds the gas tanks, diesel tanks, and, in fall and winter, the heater tanks for the house and shop. The chatty driver leaves three or four yellow invoices. Add to these the quarterly power bills, and the total each year equals more than our whole farm cost when we started farming. Kind of makes one yearn for simpler days.

From when I can first remember, Dad had a Case tractor with steel wheels that was used mainly to run the threshing machine. The rest of the farm work was done with horses. Tractor fuel then came in forty-five-gallon drums, which were laid on their sides on a stand, and the fuel transferred to the tractor by the pailful. As the barrels sometimes became rusty and occasionally were left open before they were filled, the fuel pail had a felt and brass strainer in its spout to take out water, gnats, and so on. We kids were strictly forbidden to use the fuel pails for anything at all. Gas cost only a few dollars a barrel, and the fuel pail maybe less than a dollar, but dollars were scarce.

Horse fuel didn't cost much but was "labour-intensive," to use today's jargon. Slough hay had to be cut, raked, forked onto a hayrack, forked from there onto a stack, forked from the stack to the manger, and the results forked onto a manure boat and forked out onto the fields. Oats were seeded, cut, stooked, threshed, shovelled into the chopper, the chop shovelled into a bin, then shovelled into pails and put into a chop box beside each manger, whence they found their way back to the field via the hay route.

All cooking was done on our cranky wood and coal stove. Mother was a great one for finding "meaningful labour" for us children, and she thought the wood box in the porch was a good source, not that we appreciated it that much. To chop wood, we balanced one chunk of firewood on a larger one, lifted the heavy, long-handled axe, heaved it over our heads, and slammed it down to try to make big chunks into small chunks. About every third slam, we would miss the top piece entirely and bury the axe-head in the big log. Then we had to turn it on its side so one of us could sit on it while the other wiggled the axe free. We preferred to go into the trees and glean dead branches that could be snapped into lengths with our hands or by stamping on them. But those twiggy armloads hardly lasted long enough to boil a pot of coffee in the afternoon, and we soon ran out of dead branches, anyway. We figured Mother was a bit extravagant in stoking the fire, too.

I remember a couple of trips to the pasture by the creek to pick buffalo chips. Of course, there hadn't been buffalo around since 1880, but calling the dry cow-pies "buffalo chips" seemed to make them more, well, sanitary. They were stored under an old, upturned wagon box. A small pailful would boil the kettle in no time at all. Mom insisted on using wood in the morning, however. She absolutely refused to make toast over the embers from buffalo chips. Actually, the well-sun-dried fuel was completely odour-free. It was so dry that it crumbled into dust if handled roughly. I seem to remember my little sister chewing on a chunk of it, although she denies it. She didn't report on the taste. Anyway, as she had also been caught eating garden dirt, and once chewed on an old Gillette razor blade, she couldn't be considered a gourmet. (Mother thought maybe something was lacking in her diet.)

A big, old furnace stood in the middle of the basement. Dad could bank the fire at night so it took only minutes to start warming the house in the morning. We kids used to pull on our clothes as close to the grate in the living-room as we could get. In the Thirties, however, when we couldn't afford to buy hard coal all the time, Dad would have to go for lignite coal from the mines west of Shaunavon. It was a lot harder to keep a lignite fire going overnight, and lignite coal had no redeeming quality except price.

Lignite is a soft, brown coal, halfway between hard, black coal and peat. When it was damp, it wouldn't burn; when it was dry, it was dusty and the dust was apt to explode. It produced lots of ashes and clinkers and just a little heat.

To get the lignite, Dad and Grandpa would each take two teams with wagon boxes on bobsleds and start out for the mine early in the morning. That night they stayed with relatives in Instow. The next day, they would go to the mine, pay two dollars for each wagonload, and get back as far as Scotsguard to spend the night with an aunt. On the third day, it always seemed to be blizzardy, and after dark we waited to hear the clink of harnesses and creaking of the returning sleds. We children knew how worried Mom was because she kept checking the weather and put the lamp where it could be seen from the south window until Dad arrived home, cold and tired.

The next morning, Mom laid wet cloths along the basement door sill and over the cold air ducts and braced herself to reclean everything in the basement after Dad had finished shovelling the lignite down into the coal bin.

Dad always tried to keep some hard coal for the kitchen stove, which was temperamental enough as it was. Another meaningful chore for us youngsters was filling the coal bucket. Occasionally, as we made little lumps out of big ones, we would see the tracing of fossil leaves and ferns on the face of the layers where the big lumps split.

We had one Aladdin gas lamp that was entirely Dad's responsibility to fill and light. It hung on a long hook over the table and gave bright white light from the fragile ash mantles. A couple of other lamps burned kerosene, which we called "coal oil." Every morning, "perfect housekeepers" filled the bowls, trimmed the wicks so they would burn evenly, and washed and polished the glass chimneys. As soon as Mom dared to let us kids handle the smelly coal oil and the very breakable chimneys, we had another meaningful chore.

We really didn't spend a lot of money on heat and power on the farm in those days, but we made up for that by spending a lot of man and woman power, and even child power. Looking back, simpler times were not all that simple, were they? I guess we will just keep on paying the power and fuel bills at our house.

HORSEPOWER

Four-legged, horse-power friends with personality

Our farm isn't big, but even so, we have three tractors—four, actually, if I count the garden tractor I use to cut the grass. We own four trucks in various states of health, plus a van. Add the combine, and gas motors for augers and such, as well as an assortment of electric motors, and you come up with quite a bit of horsepower. These artificial horses are convenient and efficient but often become contrary and need tender loving care, sort of like the real thing. We don't have to store hay or grind oats or give them shots. We just fill the bulk tanks with fuel and the shop with tools. We don't have to clean up after them with a pitchfork, but we need lots of grease rags, and there is always the problem of disposing of used oil and bald tires. And when they no longer meet our needs, we trade them off or junk them with never a backward glance. They just don't have much personality, not like the four-legged horsepower I used to know.

There was Nellie. When I was little, I thought the song "The Old Grey Mare" was written about her. She was more white than grey, and a little stiff in the joints, and her obsession was motherhood. Several of her children worked with Dad in the field, but Nellie was sort of retired. She pulled the garden cultivator and the buggy. We girls sometimes rode her to the pasture to get the cows. In her old age, she came back from the community pasture with a newborn colt. No, it wasn't her own—its mother had died—but Nellie adopted it and fiercely rejected any attempt by other mares, or the men at the pasture, to take it away from her. Of course she had no milk for it, though, so by the time the pair came home, the baby was in pretty poor shape. We tried to bottle-feed it, but the colt eventually died. Nellie didn't last long afterward. I was sure she had died of a broken heart.

Her daughter Queen was dark and stolid, good-tempered and just a mite lazy. Dad occasionally had to poke her in the rump with the fork handle to remind her that she was expected to pull her weight. When our town cousins wanted a horseback ride, Dad trusted Queen to carry them. They would command "Giddy-up!" and prod her sides with their heels until she broke into a slow, clumpy trot for a minute or so and then reverted to the steady plod that was her preferred gait. We kids played hide and seek in the barn and crawled under her legs in perfect safety.

Her occasional teammate, Spark Plug, was my favourite to ride when I had to get the cows. He had more energy, or at least was willing to use it. On one occasion, the cattle had wandered north into a neighbour's stubble field. On the way home, they decided to cross a rickety barbwire fence that was half-covered in blow-dirt. When Spark Plug and I followed them, he caught his left hind leg under the barbed wire, and before I knew it, I was down and so was he, with the wire cutting into his leg, unable to rise. We were too far from the yard for me to leave him and get help, so I found two rocks, put one under the wire, and pounded it with the other until the wire broke and his leg was freed. Spark Plug didn't panic at all; he just looked back over his shoulder and calmly watched the procedure. I led him home—by this time the cows were nearly there— and Dad doctored up the cut with Rawleigh's Carbolic Salve, his remedy for most everything.

Dad didn't believe in saddles, especially where we kids were concerned. If we fell off, we fell off, but at least we wouldn't be caught and dragged. Except for that time with Spark Plug, I was only ever thrown from one other horse, my brother's pony, Teddy. He was as round as a barrel and

Queen and Nellie ready to give Mom and Eileen a ride in the cutter, 1927

had no shoulders when he put his head down. He bucked me off once when I was helping Dad break him to ride, and I fell off once when my sister startled him with a swat. He headed for the barn, made a quick turn to get through the gate, and I didn't make the turn. Teddy was also the rascal that caught the loose seat of my ski pants between his teeth when I leaned over his manger looking for eggs. He didn't hurt me—just lifted me a few inches off the ground and held me there, kicking and yelling, for a couple of minutes. He thought it a lot funnier than I did, I'm sure.

By 1940 tractors were replacing horses for most field work. That summer Dad realized he was one horse short of enough teams to handle the racks for the threshing machine. He found a horse for sale at a neighbour's place three miles across country. He paid only five or ten dollars for it, and when we went over to fetch it, the reason was apparent. A more sorry, scrawny horse I had never seen. It looked half-starved. I was supposed to ride it home—no saddle, of course. It was like sitting on the narrow edge of a two-by-four. Dick—that was his name—just walked (I don't think he had enough energy to do anything else), sort of a stilted, jerky walk that jounced me with every step. I was in pain when, about halfway home, we went through a neighbour's yard. The woman came out of the house to chat, and invited me inside for a cold drink. I knew if I ever got off, I'd never have the spunk to get back on. I could scarcely even sit there and be polite. We finally continued on our way. About half a mile from home I did get off. I wasn't sure that I could walk, but I was sure I couldn't ride one more step. I told Dad that even if he got Dick for nothing, he had still been taken. By autumn, however, with proper food and some TLC, Dick turned out to be a pretty good horse. His two-by-four spine nearly disappeared under good, solid flesh but I never got on him again.

We wouldn't consider farming with horses now, as we need all the mechanical horsepower we can get. But you know what? I still miss my old one-horsepower friends. Nellie, Queen, Spark Plug, Oogie, Pete, Mike, Teddy, Star, Dick—how the names bring back old days.

OLD FRIENDS

A story about hunger and heartbreak

In the early winter of 1937, the year I was eleven, Dad decided that the fodder for the animals would not keep them all through the winter. He had travelled eight miles to harvest and bring home a stack of Russian thistle, a poor feed at best. He'd received some hay bales as relief, but these turned out to be mouldy in the middle. A few bushels of oats were left over from earlier years. The only cattle that were left were a couple of milk cows and their calves. He had sold the rest because of the drought. So many farmers had done the same thing that, after deducting the freight, Dad was lucky to get a couple of dollars for each—not even enough to buy feed for the few he kept.

Horses usually foraged for most of the winter, but this year there was no grass, not even weeds. A plague of army worms had crept across our vicinity, devouring every green thing in their path. They were so thick that the CPR train stalled on tracks that were slimy with their dead bodies, and sand had to be spread on the rails to provide enough traction for the train to move. They were so relentless in their march that they crawled up one side of the house, across the roof, and down the other. No green thing survived their passage.

Pete and Mike, the oldest team, were the worst off. They nearly quit trying to find anything, just hung around the barn, growing thinner and weaker every day. Dad had raised them from colts, and they had helped to cultivate the land, haul stones, seed, and harvest the crop for years. They were old friends.

Early one sunny morning, Dad hooked Spark Plug and Oogie to the lumber wagon and tied Pete and Mike behind. He came to the house to get the Winchester .32 rifle and a couple of bullets. He told me to dress warmly, as he would need me to hold the team.

I loved going anywhere with Dad, and I chattered as we slowly made our way across the lightly snow-covered field to Eden Coulee, about a mile away. When we got there, Dad told me to stand in the front of the wagon box, hold the reins taut, and talk to Spark Plug and Oogie so they wouldn't run away. He went to the back of the box. Two shots rang out. My team startled and pricked up their ears, but they were well trained and didn't move.

Dad got out, untied the ropes, took the halters off Pete and Mike, and got back into the wagon box. He moved slowly, like an old man. He took the reins from me, gave them a twitch, and we started home. Neither of us said a word. I kept glancing up into his face. It was expressionless, but his eyes glistened bright with unshed tears.

THE ICE HOUSE

When the fridge was an
icebox, and ice cream
meant ICE cream

One morning—early—the power went off in our area for nearly an hour. No big deal, really. I heard the computer's backup battery beeping, and I got up at about a quarter to five to phone the power company. We lit candles. Ev went to the shop to get the propane heater. It was the coldest night we have had this year, but there was very little wind, so the house didn't cool off too quickly. We have kerosene heaters and two lamps, as well as a campstove for cooking. Long experience has taught us well. We are nearly as well prepared for winter emergencies as our parents were before electricity came to the countryside.

It would be another matter if we lost power for very long in the summer. We really depend on the fridge and the freezers, and I'm not sure if I would survive without the air conditioner when the temperature gets tropical. Everything that my mother used to put up in sealers, we store away in the freezers—four of them. My parents coped very well. They had an ice house.

The ice house was a grey, shingled building with a shed roof and a trapdoor in the floor. It stood above a hole in the earth, about eight by ten feet and I suppose seven feet deep. Every winter Dad and some neighbours each took a team and low bobsled to Haakenson's dam when the ice got to about fifteen inches thick. They made a starting hole in the ice with a pick and then, using a coarsely serrated ice saw about five feet long with a crosswise handle on top, sawed the ice into foot-wide strips. As the strips were cut, one man would chip off a large block. Another stood ready to grab it with heavy tongs and pull it away from the hole as it popped above the surface . Several other men hauled the blocks up the plank ramp onto the bobsleds. I often held the team, and sometimes also my breath, scared that somebody would slip on the wet ice and fall in. Nobody ever did.

Load after load was hauled home. Dad had pulled the shed away from the hole with the team ahead of time. A pile of dry sawdust was ready to pack around and between the layers of ice blocks, both for insulation and to make the blocks easier to separate when we had to get them out. A last layer of sawdust and then the shed would be hauled back on top, and banked with earth. Not just a shed anymore, it was transformed into an ice house.

I remember one warm October day when Dad was getting the hole ready for the next crop of ice. The shed had been moved and he was down in the hole, shovelling out the damp sawdust left over from summer. All of a sudden he gave a great yell and, ignoring the ladder he had climbed down on, put his hands on the edge of the hole and leapt out in one mighty bound. He danced and jumped around, yelled a few Norwegian words, and flapped the legs of his overalls until a salamander flipped out on the ground. I guess when Dad disturbed its chosen winter hidey-hole, it decided to migrate to more peaceful territory. Dad was still wearing his summer underwear, which was actually last winter's woollen underwear with the arms and legs cut off. He didn't know his personal territory had been invaded until the cold, damp salamander crept to the top of his gartered stockings. Carolie and I were astounded at Dad's athletic ability. I think he was, too.

Dad built us an icebox, which stood in the closed-in porch all summer. He lined it with galvanized tin, insulated it, and added a layer of heavy, blue building paper, then finished the outside with V-joint boards. There were two wooden shelves inside, a galvanized tray he had soldered together at the top to hold the ice, a copper drainpipe leading out the back wall, and black hinge latches on the insulated door. Our cream, milk, and butter stayed cool and fresh inside.

Every three days, somebody had to climb down through the trapdoor in the ice house floor with a tub, break loose a big chunk of ice, and heave it up and out, leaving wet, sawdusty footprints. Carolie and I used the shed as a playhouse, too, so we were always sweeping the floor. The ice chunk was washed clean and carefully lowered into the icebox tray, making sure that the chunk didn't fall in and break loose the whole works, tray and all. That would wreck everything. A side benefit was the Virginia creeper that, nourished by the steady drip from the copper tube, grew lush and green up and over the porch wall.

On birthdays or Sundays when company was expected, we would make ice cream. I remember the recipe: a quart of skim milk, a quart of heavy cream, two small cups of sugar, a pinch of salt, four eggs, and a teaspoonful each of vanilla and maple flavouring. We would beat everything to a froth, put it into the steel inner can, assemble the beater and lid, set it into the wooden pail, attach the crank, and then pack in the ice that had been crushed into chips by pounding it in a gunny sack with the flat side of an axe. We layered in a couple of tablespoons of coarse salt to every couple of inches of ice. The little ones fought for the chance to turn the handle at first, but the glamour of that task soon wore off and we older kids earned our treat. When the turning got too hard for us, Dad would take over to make sure it was frozen enough, then drain off the brine, remove the beater, reassemble the lid and crank, and pack in more ice and salt. It was covered with an old quilt until it was time to eat. Nothing, absolutely nothing since, has ever tasted so good.

LONG JOHN LINGERIE

Underwear was cozy and warm—and we hated it

I really envy kids today. Oh, I know it's not all roses and rock music, but my grandkids certainly have smooth sailing in the matter of underwear.

I remember when there were only five fabrics: linen, cotton, wool, rayon, and silk. Linen was for tablecloths; rayon was weak and touchy to iron; silk was rare and expensive. That left cotton and wool. Wool was a touchy material, too. Washed in overly warm water, it shrank; too much rubbing, it felted; when wet, it stretched; when dry, it itched. We wore woollen mittens, scarves, sweaters, coats, and ski pants, but thankfully, the only woollen underwear belonged to Dad.

Underwear was worn for insulation, not fashion, back then. It was serious business, and nothing was more serious than getting Dad's woollen long johns off the clothesline in the middle of winter without cracking them in two. After wrenching off frozen clothespins with numb fingers, it seemed nearly as easy to wrestle a sheet of quarter-inch plywood up the stairs and in through the door, as to manoeuvre that awkward underwear into the house. It seemed to sprout extra sets of frozen legs and arms on the way in.

My sister and I and, as far as I knew, every kid who attended our country school wore cotton, fleece-lined underwear. At least we wore them until we were old enough to mount a successful rebellion. In those days, girls never wore slacks to school. We wore heavy melton-cloth ski pants on the way to and from school, and long, brown cotton stockings covered our legs in between times. I suppose we could consider ourselves lucky they weren't long, woollen stockings.

Our stockings were carefully rolled up over the fleecy underwear. They didn't look too bad on Mondays, because the extra bit of cloth on the underwear legs could be neatly folded behind the calf. By the end of the week, however, each underwear leg had stretched wide enough to accommodate an elephant. It was impossible to hide the lumps and bulges, and our vanity suffered!

At least we were spared the indignity and inconvenience of a three-button trapdoor seat. After about the second washing, one or the other of the side buttons was usually loose or missing, and the middle button was nearly impossible to do up in the first place. Now our underwear had a vertical, lapped opening with only one button. This made for quite a bit of tension every time we bent over, and the buttonhole often became so stretched that it wouldn't stay done up. As we were also forced to wear sturdy bloomers on top of our underwear, with elastic at the waist and legs, that button wasn't too essential.

We wore flannelette undervests, called "waists," to which we attached our garters. (When we were young, we called them "corsets" because our mother wore corsets. We were humiliated when our cousins laughed at us, but we had become so accustomed to the name, it was difficult to remember to say "waist.") Inch-wide elastics, with a gripper at the end, were attached with safety pins and each week transferred to a fresh waist. They didn't exactly keep our stockings taut and sleek, but at least they kept them from collapsing around our ankles.

I'm sure my grandchildren would throw a fit if they had to wear the same underclothes all week. Maybe if they had to carry every drop of wash water in and out of the house, and scrub their clothes by hand, their standards would drop a bit. Never mind the grandchildren. If I still had to do all that, I would be a lot stingier about laundry, myself!

I don't suppose we suffered that much, because everybody we knew wore heavy underwear all winter. As far as smell went, anyone who went to a country school knows that most of us usually had colds and couldn't smell anything, and if we could, the odour of chalk, orange peelings, and Dustbane was pervasive enough to make anything else just a minor nuisance.

Still, I kind of envy today's youngsters. Pantyhose, tights, and synthetic fabrics are a great improvement on the "good old days." I have no nostalgia at all when it comes to fleece-lined lingerie.

WINTER CHORES

Deep snow
and making memories

The Christmas cards sit in a basket on the coffee table. Soon I'll bundle them up and tuck them away until next year. I reread the enclosed Christmas letters and notes that bring news from family and friends, musing about other places, other years.

I look at the old-fashioned pictures: high-stepping horses pulling light sleighs filled with huge-skirted women and fancy-hatted men on their way to a window-bright church, past snow-covered cottages where carollers sing. Snowflakes speckle the scene, in spite of the clear, star-filled, navy blue sky. And then I think, Christmas cards are such fibs! Maybe winter just isn't the same as in the good old days. I bet it never was.

Sixty years ago, winter was hard on animals and on the people who looked after them. Dad always had slough hay and oat bales stacked behind the barn, and a granary of oats to be made into chop. As well, a pile of wheat straw had been threshed into the stack yard in the fall for bedding. Other straw piles stood in the fields, left as shelter for some of the horses that weren't used much in winter. They were allowed the freedom of the fenced farm, where they got most of their food by pawing away at the snow-covered sloughs, supplemented by whatever hay Dad could spare.

Except for the milk cows and small calves, the cattle were kept in the barnyard or the "close" pasture, near shelter from the wind. Cattle were not as adept as horses at foraging, so they had to be fed extra hay in the barnyard.

Water was in chronic shortage on our farm. The windmill well in the yard could never keep up with the demand of the twenty or so cattle and the chore team over winter. As cattle, unlike horses, couldn't get enough water from eating snow, Dad let the cows out of the barn every morning, called the rest of the cattle with "Coo-boss, Coo-boss" through the megaphone of his cupped hands, and herded them to the dugout in Grandpa's pasture or, if that was nearly dry, to another dugout more than half a mile away. I said herded, but actually the cattle knew quite well what was up. They trailed along behind Dad, who rode the stoneboat pulled by the chore team, Spark Plug and Oogie. Dad chopped a hole in the ice with an axe that was fastened to a thong tied to his arm, so that if it slipped from his mittened hands, it wouldn't be lost down the hole. After he scooped out the ice chips, the cattle would crowd around and drink their fill, sometimes coming back for a second or third helping. Then the team drank while the cattle started for home, where they knew fresh hay would be served.

On nice days my sister and I tied our sleds behind the stoneboat and went along to "help." I can't imagine what help we could have been, but Dad enjoyed having us along.

There were also miserable days, when the wind howled, the snow obliterated anything more than four or five feet away, and the red in the thermometer disappeared into the bulb. Then the milk cows and the chore horses would drink from the ice-rimmed trough beside the well and be let back into the barn. The other cattle would then be allowed to drink until the well ran dry. They never got enough on those days and had to chomp down some snow to be satisfied.

Milking had to be done as close to twelve-hour intervals as possible, so morning chores were always finished by the time we were up and dressed. On nice evenings we often went with Dad to the barn. Our long-legged shadows danced to the swing of the coal-oil lantern he carried, and the frosty air nipped our nostrils. The soft lantern light didn't dim the stars that hung like glitter on a blue velvet canopy.

Dad hung the lantern on a hook between the stalls. We girls took our smaller forks and helped clean up the stalls, spreading fresh straw as bedding. Then we made our way to the animals to dole out a dipperful of chop for each one. After we learned how to milk, we would set up the stool and milk pail, snug our toqued heads into the flank of a cow, and try to imitate the long, strong rhythm that Dad made as he filled two milk pails to our half one. The cows munched and snorted, their warm cow breath wafting back to us. We squirted milky sprays into the mouths of barnyard cats that waited beside a dented aluminium pan for their share of fresh milk. We learned to be quick on the trigger, grabbing the pail and stool and backing up quickly when our friend humped her back and shuffled her hind legs, warnings that the golden stream was about to flow.

After separating, Dad carried the extra warm skim milk back to the barn to feed the calves. We girls were glad to be back in the warm house. We had no idea how fortunate we were to be tucking away so many memories. Saskatchewan winters were hard on humans and animals, but I wouldn't trade my memories for all the Christmas-card winters in the world.

WE COULD LISTEN TO THE WORLD

When radio
came into our lives

Radio was invented quite a while before I was, but I must have been about five before I heard one. Uncle Arvid had got hold of a black Bakelite receiver, about three feet wide and a foot high, that had a slanted front on which were three black, knurled knobs. A set of earphones came with it. The men passed the earphones back and forth and twiddled the tuner knobs. The women were busy making dinner. They ignored the men and their new toy. We cousins were allowed a quick listen, but all I heard were squeals and a whooshy sound. The part of the day that I remember most clearly is when Uncle lined us up, all holding hands, grabbed a hand at one end, and touched a little silver hole in the radio. We all got a shock, especially the kid at the far end of the line.

Several years later Dad brought home a large, brown cabinet radio, with two swing doors that closed to protect the grey-brocade-covered speaker. We had no electricity, so our radio was powered by a small, square, red "C" battery, two rectangular, blue "B" batteries, and the "A" battery that was just an ordinary black job like the battery in the Model T. The "A" battery kept running out of juice, as Dad called it, so he had to improvise a way of charging it.

He either carved or found a propeller blade about three feet across. It was mounted on top of the cook car, and Dad hooked it to a six-volt generator that he scrounged from an old car. When the wind blew, he was in business with his home-made battery charger. When the radio volume faded to faint murmurs, Dad would replace the weak battery with the charged battery and hook the invalid up for its turn at the juice hospital.

Radios also needed antennae, or aerials. This was usually a long wire, connected to boards nailed to the eaves and stretch-ing across the roof. Fastened on with insulators, it continued down the side of the house, through one of the round holes in the storm window vent, under the sash, and was wound around a screw on the back of the radio. That procedure insured that the radio stayed wherever it was first put, although it was too bulky to move on a whim, anyway. There was an indoor version of the antenna (Uncle Garry had one), a cross-shaped thing mounted on a base, with wire strung round and round on the arms in concentric squares. I meddled with it once and put it out of sync, resulting in a good deal of commotion, and I got bawled out by everyone around.

It wasn't everyone who had a radio in those days. I remem-ber a couple of neighbours who usually came to visit the nights the prize fights were on. Some people were said to string up an antenna on top of the house, just to make others think they had a radio. I doubt that, because every radio needed a two-dollar licence and the antenna would alert the authorities. Two dollars doesn't sound like much now, but then it would buy forty ice cream cones, or twenty quarts of milk, or ten pairs of socks, or a two-year subscription to the *Free Press Prairie Farmer*. A bit too steep if the only object was prestige.

Batteries were expensive, and one set of "B"s and "C"s was expected to last at least a year, so the radio was turned on only when one was prepared to listen, never just for back-ground noise as it often is today. I would have been shocked if someone had told me then that today, on our farm, there would be seven radios in the house, one in each of the vehi-cles, including the tractors, as well as a couple of portables that clamp on over the head like the old earphones did. And only four ears between us to listen to them!

FRESH BREAD

When "home-made" bread was nothing special

I have an automatic breadmaker on my kitchen counter. I got it for Christmas a couple of years ago, and at the time, I really thought I wanted it. No, it was more than that: I needed it. I had visions of a fresh loaf of bread every day—eating it, smelling it. Nothing, except for home-made chili sauce bubbling on the stove, sets the tastebuds tingling like the smell of bread baking in the oven.

I don't use the breadmaker as often as I should. For one thing, the bread doesn't make good toast, so there goes our main bread event of the day. Plus I'm never sure, when I set the breadmaker going, that I'll still be in the house when the bread is ready. Our days are often filled with spur-of-the-moment jaunts to Moose Jaw for the mail, business stuff, or groceries; or else the neighbours spontaneously invite us over for a cup of coffee. Sometimes we hop in the truck to check the crops or to take a look-see at a "maybe prehistoric" carving on a stone in someone's pasture. But the main reason I don't often use the breadmaker is I like making bread and buns the manual way, and I always make a triple recipe, as much as my big, old bread pan will hold. With quick yeast, I'm finished in only about six hours. There are usually home-made buns in the freezer, and my ego soars when I bring them out and hear the oohs and aahs.

When I was a kid, there was no quick yeast—or any other shortcut. Mothers stayed home a lot more, too. Baking was scheduled for Tuesdays, when the stove had to be fired up all day anyway to heat the sad-irons to iron Monday's washing. Bread making started Monday evening, when a square, dry cornmeal yeast cake was soaked in lukewarm sugar water until it was frothy. Then the "sponge" was made with sugar, salt, lard, lukewarm water, flour, and the bubbly yeast. The water usually included the liquid that the potatoes had been boiled in, as well as a cupful of mashed potatoes. Only half of the recipe's total flour was put into the sponge to make it stirrable, about the consistency of cake-mix dough. After it was well beaten, the sponge was put into a *very* big bowl, covered, and wrapped in blankets to keep warm for the night. The yeast multiplied, feeding on the sugar and flour, and the whole works doubled or tripled in volume—hence the *very* big bowl. Next morning the rest of the flour was kneaded in, and after the dough rose twice and was punched down each time, the dough was formed into loaves and put into pans. When the loaves doubled in size, they were ready for the oven.

Nowadays I get the oven ready by turning two knobs. Mom's old stove took a lot more finesse. The insulation around the oven had burned away on one side, so the fire had to be mostly embers with a little sprinkle of fresh coal on top to keep the temperature even and avoid sudden flare-ups during baking. The temperature gauge on the oven door was unreliable, but Mom, from long experience, could tell if it was hot enough by putting her hand inside for a few seconds. Even at that, the loaves usually burnt a bit on one side before the other side was done. We kids became expert at hiding little rinds of burnt crust under the edges of our plates, next to our stomachs.

An alternative to dried cornmeal yeast cakes was to put a fist-sized chunk of uncooked bread dough into the flour bin. It dried on the outside but the yeast stayed alive inside the lump. When soaked in warm water for the next baking session, the yeast reactivated. Our neighbour, Mrs.

THE SEWING MACHINE

*An old Singer machine brings
back some painful memories*

It's odd how an item will often trigger a train of memory. We were having coffee with our neighbours and, as it was spring, the talk turned to auction sales. They had a flyer about a sale south of Cadillac. The people selling out happened to be my third cousins. We decided to go, not that we intended to buy anything, as we're at the stage where we're trying to unload stuff, not collect more. It would be a good chance to meet lots of old friends, and it was. Some of the old friends were people and some were the items to be sold.

I almost changed my mind about buying. One of the objects listed among the "numerous household articles" was a Singer sewing machine so old that rather than fold down into a console, the black machine adorned with a golden sphinx was covered when not in use by a veneered wooden box. My mind flashed back to Grandma's kitchen table, where I often saw her mending shirts or hemming pillowcases with her Singer. That old machine didn't even have a treadle; there was a handle to crank on the flywheel. One hand was always busy turning the machine, leaving her only one hand to control the material. I wonder that she managed—I sometimes wish for a third hand just to keep the material where I want it. When Grandma finished her mending, she covered the little portable with its wooden case and stored it in her closet.

Mom's sewing machine was more modern, if less than

efficient. Dad had bought it at an auction sale. It was a treadle machine that folded down into a console with two long, narrow drawers on each side and a small tip-out drawer across the front. When Dad brought it home, he discovered the working parts didn't—work, that is. It was full of rust. He dismantled it and soaked everything in kerosene for a few days. When every piece was clean and shiny again, he put it back together. And it worked. Well, it worked in sort of a cranky way. Mother said she thought it was the same machine Mrs. Noah had used to mend Noah's pants.

Mom struggled with that machine for twenty years. She hadn't learned to sew when she was a girl. A lot of her sewing was making over things that we had been given through relief boxes or hand-me-downs from relatives, and she cut out the pieces according to instinct; paper patterns were too expensive to buy. Most of her sewing was done by guess and by gosh. She had black thread for dark material and white for everything else, and it was all size thirty—pretty thick thread but the only size that worked in her machine. Under the circumstances, she accomplished miracles.

I learned to sew on that machine. I had a doll named Jane, the nicest one I ever had, with a kid-skin body and a china head. I made Jane dresses and coats and hats and underwear using bits and pieces from remnants and the rag bag. About the only instruction I heard was "Don't sew your finger." I guess I couldn't really damage the machine.

After we were married, I borrowed Ev's mother's treadle Singer until we could afford one of our own. I have always had to sew most of my own clothes, mainly because I am so tall that ready-made clothing just doesn't fit. I could have been wearing mini-skirts long before they were fashionable. On my old treadle machine, I made a lot of my kids' clothing, drapes, and bedspreads, and I even occasionally mended binder canvas. It was a tough old girl.

What a thrill when rural electricity came to our area and I became the owner of an electric sewing machine! It had buttonhole makers and fancy stitches built right in. It could zigzag and even go in reverse. My boys got matching shirts; Karen got fancy velvet dresses; Ev and his dad were supplied with Western shirts; I made quilts. About the only thing I didn't try was blue jeans. Oh, I could have taken a class to learn how to make them, but I didn't take it. I realized that anything I knew how to do, I ended up *having* to do, so I drew the line at blue jeans.

I got to thinking I was pretty clever. One day, I was making something that needed a zipper. I had just finished zigzagging all the raw edges and then placed the zipper just so, holding it close to the needle with pins and fingers instead of basting. After all, I must have put in three hundred zippers over the years. No problem. I stepped firmly on the control. The first stitch went just where it was supposed to go. The second stitch jumped sideways and went through my finger, nail and all. I had forgotten to take the machine out of zigzag mode. The stem of the needle stayed in the machine; the point, complete with thread, broke off under my finger; and the middle part was firmly imbedded in flesh. I tried to pull it out. No luck. I hollered for my son Lyle. He had been too sick to go to school and was downstairs in bed. He came up, sat me down in a chair, and then galloped in bare feet and shorts across the yard to the shop to get some pliers.

It turned out okay. Lyle pulled out the steel and put a bandage on, and it healed up without any infection. But I didn't feel so clever any more. Imagine, forgetting the first and best sewing instruction I ever got: "Don't sew your finger!"

GARDEN HELP

The joys of helping and being helped

A backyard garden in town is often the pride and joy of the man of the family, but here on the farm a garden usually is (and was) considered a woman's domain. You may be "closer to God in a garden than any place on Earth," but most farmers would rather do their meditating on a four-wheel-drive tractor pulling a sixty-foot cultivator than holding a hoe. And usually the farm wife is just as happy if her husband makes his contribution to horticulture by seeing that the oil is changed and the dirt rinsed out of the filter of the air cleaners on the rototillers and mowers.

The rototiller is about the handiest hired help a woman can have. It sure beats the way the garden was cultivated way back when. I remember leading Nellie out between rows of potatoes while Dad handled the little cultivator she pulled. Nellie was reliable, gentle, and willing, but she swung her front feet out a bit with each step and managed to land her big foot on my sneaker-clad toe a couple of times each row. It didn't hurt much because the ground was soft, but something like that does make a kid remember cultivating potatoes. I really enjoy my mechanical help. Years ago I developed great shoulders doing the spring tilling of the garden, potato patch, newly planted trees, and rows of bushes with my trusty rototiller. Ev even suggested that I was welcome to start on the summer fallow if I ran out of smaller plots.

For years we didn't have a reliable water source, so I planted garden rows wide apart and weeded them with the tiller. With a little finesse, it can clean out weeds right up to the row. Tiller finesse is not a strong point of someone used to operating big machines, so masculine help was usually politely declined. Maybe it isn't just the big machines that cause the problem. Dad's weren't that big, and I remember him cleaning out Mom's newly planted rows of asparagus roots four years in a row before she gave up on them.

I like sitting between the rows to pick the weeds between the plants. It is peaceful, a good time to daydream and plan or occasionally to reconstruct arguments that didn't turn out right when they were actually happening. I am very witty, sitting alone in the garden. And when the kids got old enough to help, it was a good place to have heart-to-heart talks. Young kids are happy to help. Once they get older, they find out that it is actually work. Too young is risky, though. My granddaughter Lynn, at two and a half, was enthusiastic, so I explained several times that corn was the good plant and everything else wasn't, and showed her the difference. She made quick progress down her row—too quick, it seemed. Lynn had grasped the difference but didn't get the fundamental idea. I ran over to find her diligently removing the "good" ones. She hadn't missed a plant.

We water from the well now, so my much-smaller garden has rows that are close together. Every sunny morning I saunter out to see what progress has occurred overnight and do a bit of hoeing while I am there. It is a lovely way to start the day. With only two of us to feed now, I do not can, freeze, and pickle the amounts I used to, but nothing can match the flavour of fresh strawberries, baby carrots, and rosy little potatoes—not to mention corn on the cob picked just before dinner.

Every year one or two of the things I plant suddenly go crazy, and I end up with an over-abundance of tomatoes, or beets, or spaghetti squash. When unwary neighbours come over I unload my surplus on them, whether they want it or not. Sometimes I appreciate that kind of help more than any other kind. Not only do I get credit for being generous, but I also do not have to can, freeze, or pickle anything for a while.

Hauling hay

UNTO THE THIRD AND FOURTH GENERATION

Words from our heritage

It is not only the result of sin that continues to bedevil children unto the third and fourth generation (Deut: 5:9 and Exodus 20:5). At least not in our family. We have words that do the same thing.

My paternal grandparents were staunch, upright, loyal Christians of the upright and loyal Norwegian Lutheran persuasion. Because Grandma acted as if she believed that God was also a staunch, upright, loyal Norwegian Lutheran, she also seemed to think that the Norwegian language was God's native tongue (after all, her Bible was written in Norwegian) and just a mite holier than, say, English. Many of her peers were of the same opinion. As a result, until I was about eight, services in our local country church were held only in Norwegian.

Our parents, who had weathered the stress of being introduced to the English language in the first grade at school, spoke English at home to prevent us from going through the same trauma. Grandma, however, spoke to us in Norwegian, we answered in English (which she understood), and it was an impasse. As a result, though, we older grandchildren became auditorially bilingual, if there is such a thing. We sat through the church services, learned the Lord's Prayer and the Apostles' Creed by rote, and tried to sing along as Dad pointed to the words in the

Norwegian hymnal. We were confused until we figured out that we should pronounce every "f" as an "s," but we still didn't quite understand what we were singing or saying.

Some of those Norwegian words had a sonorous ring that seemed just right for church. Words like "forladelse" and "kjødets opstandelse" or "evige liv." I was a little dubious about "hellig" because it sounded like a forbidden word, and I felt just a little disappointed when I found out it meant "holy," not "hellish."

If Norwegian was the holy language, it was also the profane. Dad never swore in front of children or women— nor anywhere else usually. Still, no one who has had to cope with the denseness of farm animals or the perversity of machinery could judge him harshly if they found him using emphatic Norwegian on occasion. Those words were never translated for us by the adults, but we soon caught on, and to this day I possess a small Norwegian vocabulary of the profane and scatological.

Our parents did use other words and phrases to us and at us that seem so apt and untranslatable that they also became part of our heritage. A baby cooing, or a child who tried not to cry when actual blood was seeping from a scrape, or any freshly bathed toddler tucked into bed was a "stakkar liten." We interpreted this as "dear little one." When we finished our meal, we said to the cook, "Takk for mat," and she replied, "Vær så god," which approximated "thanks" and "you're welcome." If we became overly noisy, we were told to be "tyst still," and we had to tame down, tone down, ease up, or shut up, depending on the tone of voice.

After church, we took off our "hærdags" clothes and put on "hverdags" to play. When we were required to do errands, our mother said she needed a "spring poik" or "jump-boy" (I think a bit of Swedish crept in there). If we were reluctant to "spring poik," we were told that we could not "dor sticka e course," which meant that we were too lazy to make a cross of two sticks. The logic of crossing two sticks escaped us then, and still does me today, but I would just as soon not be told I was incapable of doing it.

About the worst expression was "slusket." Being care-
less was "slusket." Spilling was "slusket." Not finishing a
task, such as dusting or washing dishes properly, was
"slusket." Dirty faces and tangled hair were "slusket."
Untied shoelaces and droopy socks were "slusket," as was
a slatternly housekeeper. It was not our favourite word.

We, the grandchildren then, are grandparents now. None
of our children or grandchildren have spoken anything but
English in their lives—except for those useful and untranslatable bits and pieces of Norwegian and Swedish that are
visited unto the third and fourth generation.

Our grandchildren know what it means to run to the
basement as a "spring poik." They tone down when they
hear "tyst still," and change into "hverdags" clothing
when they get home. They have all been told at one time
or another that they cannot cross two sticks and know
that they must shape up when they are "slusket." I am
pretty sure their children will hear the same expressions.
After all, why discard a useful inheritance?

LITTLE HEDGE ON THE PRAIRIE

Pioneer faith and the buildings that housed it

Every summer we go back to visit the community where I grew up. The hills where we used to go tobogganing are not as high as they were when I was little, nor are the creeks as wide or the sloughs as deep. It's more lonesome than it used to be. I pick out old landmarks like the place where Albert Elton lived, and Pete Randclev's place. Uncle Oliver's trees are there, just across from our old gate. Clumps of trees mark the homes where neighbours lived on half-section farms. "Trees" I say because most of them are homes no more. There once were trees around every home, but often only the outer caragana hedges remain to barricade groups of granaries from fierce winds that charge across the prairie. Caraganas, the scraggly survivors of history.

When Minnesota was opened to settlement 140 years ago, many Scandinavian immigrants took homesteads around Pelican Rapids. My great-great-grandfather and many of his relatives and friends took up land west of town in an area they called "Norwegian Grove." As soon as they could, they built Immanuel Lutheran Church, a white, wooden church with a tall spire and bell tower, in a grove of pines. Pastors were recruited from Norway. Soon the rolling churchyard started to fill up with loved ones buried under headstones inscribed with Bible verses and hymns, as well as names and dates—all in Norwegian script.

Later, when the Norwegian American Synod was established, some members of Immanuel were loath to leave their Norwegian Synod roots. A few families even split up over the issue. Great-great-grandfather Johannes, his wife, and some of their children enlisted in the faction that joined the American Synod. His eldest son, my great-grandfather Ole Jacob, and his family stayed put with the old Norwegian Synod. The breakaways erected a copy of the old church, complete with spire and bell tower, about a mile to the east. They claimed the name Immanuel, too, so the pair became known as East Immanuel and West Immanuel. There they sat, within sight of each other for more than fifty years, until the older church burned down. By that time, prejudices had evaporated and the congregations united.

As my father's generation neared maturity, parents in the area realized there was not enough land nearby to provide their numerous offspring with farms. They were afraid the boys would go to the city or, worse yet, head west to Montana and become wild cowboys. About that time, in the early 1900s, the Canadian government was advertising homesteads in Saskatchewan. Grandpa and several of his cousins were among many Scandinavian-Americans from that area who listened to the siren call of new land. They brought their large families to homestead on the prairie about fifty miles south of Swift Current, the nearest rail point at that time. They built homes, broke the prairie sod, and, perhaps lonesome for the groves of Minnesota or maybe even for the Norwegian forests their grandparents described, started planting and replanting trees and shelterbelts that the prairie kept killing off with drought and wind.

They also organized a church. A white, wooden building, called North Immanuel, was built in Admiral, and the sister congregation in our area ten miles away, served by the same pastor, was called South Immanuel. What with the East and West Immanuels in Minnesota, that took care of the cardinal points of the compass.

Our South Immanuel congregation met in the schoolhouse until 1933. A formal church, a white, wooden building with a spire (but no bell), was then built—a tribute to the faith and devotion of prairie people suffering through years of drought and depression. They surrounded most of the churchyard with a hedge of caragana, about the only tree that could survive at that time, and Dad brought roots of hardy lilacs from our farm to plant on the side of the yard nearest the road.

In the Thirties, the English language started to supplant Norwegian in church services on alternating Sundays. As my generation grew up, English took over, although Norwegian was still a required course in the seminary until very recently. It was in the Thirties that women were given voting privileges in church affairs. About time, too, as much of the financing of the minister's salary, furnishing the church, upkeep of the manse, and mission support was taken care of by the Ladies' Aid, who raised money with fowl suppers, community catering, and the sale of quilts and other handicrafts.

South Immanuel Church is no more. Shortly after its twenty-fifth anniversary, lightning struck the building. No one at that summer's vacation Bible school was hurt, and neighbours soon came to help carry out whatever could be saved. There was no water or firefighting equipment, so the wooden building burned to the foundation. As the community gathered the next day, people were stunned to find that midnight vandals had looted the cornerstone, which had held pictures, historical records, some personal mementoes, scripture, and a couple of dollars' worth of money samples. A poor haul for the thieves but an additional heartbreak for the congregation.

For a while, the South Immanuel congregation held on. Another church building was moved onto the foundation, but as farms grew larger, people moved to the city, and roads improved, the North and South congregations merged. A Bible camp bought the South building. Now all that's left of the place where I was confirmed and married is a square plot of land at a crossroad, bounded on three sides by caraganas with a lilac hedge at the front.

GRANDMA'S KITCHEN

A real "family room"

Grandma's kitchen was a big, square room with bright double windows to the east. Grandma's small rocker sat in front of them, where we often saw her putting the newest grandchild to sleep across her knees while her hands were busy knitting socks or mittens. The wood and coal stove, with its satellites, the coal scuttle and wood box, were ranged along the north wall. A big, round pedestal table, covered in oilcloth, nestled among varnished ladderback chairs, and on the wall behind the table, the telephone was mounted at just the right height to put a good dent in the skull of anyone getting up from the chair beneath it. In one corner, a washstand held a hand basin, waterpail and dipper, and Grandpa's shaving stuff. On the corner of the towel rack his double razor strop hung ready to hone the straight razor. Behind glass doors of a built-in cabinet, the pink-flowered dinner set and the silver spoon holder sat on shelves. Above them dainty cups hung on hooks. Under the shelves were drawers, more shelves, and a big flour bin hinged at the bottom. It was a comfortable room, where most of the family visiting took place. Baking, dishwashing, canning, and sewing had to be done on the table or stove top. Not all that convenient.

But then there was the pantry! It was about five feet by twelve, with a little north window at the far end. The cellar's

Grandpa and Grandma (Ole and Karen) Kopperud, 1937

trapdoor occupied most of the floor and opened sideways. When the door was propped open with a stick, Grandma always cautioned us not to get too close or we would fall in. The cellar held only the potato bin and shelves of canned meat, vegetables, and fruit, so one trip downstairs each day was usually sufficient.

The walls of the pantry were lined with long shelves. Grandma stored cookies, cakes, and pies there, along with leftovers to be used up in the next day or two, maybe a ham or roast, gravy, and some pickles. It always smelled so good in there.

Inside the pantry door there was a coffee grinder with a glass jar on top to hold coffee beans, and a small glass cup in a holder underneath held just the right amount of fresh-ground coffee to put into the blue and white enamel pot. Grandma always started coffee with cold water, let it barely come to a boil, poured in a "skret" of cold water to settle the grounds, and the result turned all her grandchildren into coffee addicts. Aunt Mina loved to chew freshly ground coffee and often sneaked a little from the grinder. I can still hear Grandma telling her that it would all go straight to her appendix, and that she would remember what she had been told when *that* happened.

The kitchen was usually a busy place. I went "up home," as we called Grandpa and Grandma's house, along with my dad one day, when he was going to help grind beef after butchering. The men took turns at the big, old hand-cranked meat grinder while Grandma made little meatballs and seared them in big, black frying pans. She packed them into sealers, fitted on new rubber rings, glass tops, and metal rings, and then set the jars, eighteen at a time, into an oval copper boiler to be covered with hot water and boiled for four hours. No freezers or pressure cookers in those days.

Another big job was churning cream into butter. After using a little churn that seemed to take forever to handle all the cream, they acquired a barrel churn somewhere, probably at an auction sale. It sure held a lot of cream. A foot treadle turned it, and it did look as if it would work out fine. A wooden bung in one end was supposed to be opened every few minutes to let out the gas generated by the sour cream, but nobody knew just how soon to do it. Grandpa kept treadling, the pressure built up, and the bung popped out on its own. This happened, unfortunately, when the bung was at the bottom of the rotating barrel and sour cream shot out all over the place. Grandma was not impressed.

On Sundays after church, Grandma's kitchen was often the gathering spot for all the aunts, uncles, and cousins. Meatballs and gravy, creamed peas and carrots, mounds of mashed potatoes, and beet pickles followed by crisp sugar cookies and saskatoon berries topped off with cream from the big cream jug—those meals from Grandma's pantry linger on in memory. It was a good thing that calories and cholesterol hadn't yet been invented.

After dinner, especially on stormy days when we cousins couldn't play outside, Flinch cards would appear and everyone would gather at the big table to play the noisy game. Even the toddlers sat on their parents' laps to help call for cards and yell "Flinch." Grandma didn't approve of regular cards with faces on them and coloured symbols, but Flinch cards didn't seem to have such a close connection with the Devil.

Too soon, it always seemed, Grandma would go to the pantry door, crank the coffee grinder, put the pot on the stove, and get out another plate of cookies. We had to put the games away and, after coffee, go home to do the chores. It didn't really matter. We knew that sometime soon, there would be another Sunday in Grandma's kitchen.

HEAVENLY DAYS

A humorous look into the hereafter

I have been thinking about the hereafter lately. Not that I am expecting to travel there in the near future, in spite of my young grandson, who assured me that I had three or four years left when he found out how ancient I was. No, I am pretty healthy and happy, but every once in a while, I think about heaven.

I am not too thrilled with the usual descriptions—all those streets of gold, jewelled buildings, harps and choirs, and having to wear those bed sheets that we wind the little girls into for Christmas pageants. It might be fun to visit a heaven like that as a tourist, but not for an eternity!

First of all, there are the permanent residents—heaven is said to be full of angels, archangels, seraphim (those are the six-winged variety), and cherubim. I used to think that cherubim were those little fellows with wings and a loose diaper, and I always thought they might appreciate a little rocking and cuddling, both of which I am good at, but no— they are lions with eagle wings and a human head, or is it humans with a lion's body and eagle wings? Either way, I can't see us having much to talk about, except maybe ancient Egypt or nightmares.

As for the choirs, now I love choir music, and I love singing. I am sure my mother, who also loved music and singing but couldn't hold a tune here on Earth, is in her glory. So I am all for the choirs, but a bit of variety would be nice. Sort of CBC style instead of the country music or rock stations with the same tunes played over and over.

Streets of gold! Why would we need streets anyhow? We will be able to go anywhere we want to in a sort of swoosh, in a twinkling of an eye. On second thought, maybe streets are a prerequisite for males. At least the men in our family would sure feel deprived without wheels. Houses made of jewels and ivory and marble palaces sound pretty grand, sort of like the cathedrals in England. But you would never dare to redecorate, and it would take some nerve to just take your shoes off and make yourself comfy. I think I will see if there isn't a little wooden house somewhere on a back road.

I'm not really looking for a little log cabin—maybe more of a country-inn type house, with lots of nooks and crannies, many bedrooms, and big bathrooms. *Of course* there should be bathrooms. Even if they have solved the problem of eating anything we want to and never gaining a pound or having heartburn or constipation, I still think it is a wonderful idea to have a place where one could loll around in a big tub of bubble bath, or even just a room where you could lock the door and shut everyone out for a while.

I am not sure about those white robes, either. They might be great for lounging around on the clouds, and one could conceal a lot of cellulite and legs kindly described as sturdy, but surely we will get a better deal, aesthetically, next time round. I do know that one hand would always have to be holding everything in place, and I would have to work at sitting like a lady, knees together and feet flat on the clouds. I think I would rather have some slacks and T-shirts. A few nice dresses, too. I've always wanted a real slinky dress even though I am not the slinky kind. Do you think that would be too frivolous to ask for?

No night there! How sad. I find nothing more pleasant than to crawl under the comforter, turn on the light, and read myself to sleep. No night means no sunsets, and a prairie soul would sure miss them. No stars, either, or velvet blue skies. My heaven will have to have night.

It will have to have weather, too. I'm not a fan of blizzards or hail or windstorms, but the snow on the hills, rain pattering on the roof, hoar-frost on the bushes and trees, leaves turning amber and red and brown in the fall, even the sharp smell of an approaching thunderstorm—I cherish all of these.

Of course there will be gardens, flowers, trees, and grass. And a few weeds, too. I kind of like picking weeds, except portulaca. And I want a lake with a sandy bottom, and a boat, and a place on shore for a wiener roast and a singsong. I need a library. I can't imagine being happy without books. I hope I can keep working with clay and retain the thrill of opening the kiln to see how everything came out.

There will probably be a lot of family reunions, just like we have here any chance we get. Maybe by then I will be able to sort everyone out from reading the family histories, and I will know which kid belongs to which cousin. It is going to have to be some reunion to beat the ones we have had here in Saskatchewan.

Come to think of it, my heaven is going to end up an awful lot like Saskatchewan, with better weather and fewer mosquitoes!

TEARING UP
THE TRACKS

A page of our
history vanishes

Rail companies are pulling up the tracks all over Saskatchewan. It's a pity. They claim that the web of rail lines that used to connect all the cities, towns, villages, and sidings in the west are no longer profitable. And that may be. But in the process, they are erasing another page of our history.

Like most of our first settlers, my grandfather brought his family, his livestock and machinery, the furniture, bedding, tools, and hopes for the future to the prairie on the train. They came only from as far as Minnesota, but others came from around the world: Britain, Germany, China, Ukraine, Poland, France, anywhere—everywhere. The train carried their belongings, and their stout hearts and strong backs, to the last, best west.

The summer before they immigrated, Grandpa and his cousin walked forty-some miles south from the railroad station in Swift Current to find the "land locator." He took them by horse and buggy to find suitable land to claim as their homesteads. They decided on the area now called Boule Creek. Several years later, they had built their homes, broken the sod, and raised their first crop. By then, the railhead had extended to Neville, so their first grain was hauled by horse and wagon thirty-five miles. A year later, the Assiniboia line came through Cadillac, a mere seven-mile trip from home. The web of rail spread over the south country until most farms were within ten miles of a railway station.

Monday through Saturday, the train stopped twice a day in Cadillac, eleven in the morning going east and about five in the afternoon going west. It brought the mail: newspapers, letters from family away from home, and mail-order parcels, including the vital Christmas order from Eaton's. It brought groceries to replenish the shelves of local stores, ploughs and seed drills to work the land. On its return trip, it took cans of cream and crates of eggs to city dairies. It carried cattle to be sold at city stockyards, and square, red boxcars of grain, some to supply Canadians with bread and the rest to export at the Lakehead. It brought Easterners to help with the harvest and teachers to staff the little, white country schools, and took young men and women away to college and university, or to greener pastures to look for work. In the Dirty Thirties, it brought boxcars of fish, cheese, and apples from generous donors down east. And it took thousands of our strong, young men to war in far countries, many of them never to see the West again.

On a personal note, I remember Mom occasionally setting the clock to the right time by watching for the white plume of steam across the valley at eleven o'clock. I remember Dad and the neighbours coming home all soot and ashes after putting out grass fires started by sparks from the engine or a hot box in the wheels. When I boarded in town for high school, we would often go to the station to watch the train come puffing in, hoping for a bit of excitement. It usually wasn't very exciting, but it gave us something to do in the hiatus between 3:30 and homework. I remember the apprehensive anticipation I felt when, at seventeen, I was sent off alone to Regina to go to business college. And on the long trips home on the mixed train at Christmas, the passenger cars were crowded and the freight so plentiful that the train became later and later as we stopped at each little station.

Now the local trains are nearly gone. Well, progress progresses, I guess. I don't really want to retrace our steps to the days of hauling grain in sixty-bushel wagons with a team of horses. Yet the loss of branch lines and local elevators means we're back to hauling our grain and cattle thirty-five miles to market again, at the same time pulverizing our country roads with semi-trailer traffic. Little towns are vanishing as their prairie sentinels, the grain elevators, are torn down. The sense of community is fast disappearing as big farms swallow up small ones. Neighbours are becoming scarce. And all in the name of bigger and more profitable, today's watchwords.

We farmers feel sort of ambivalent about these watchwords. We all suspect that the prairie farm is merely becoming bigger, and it is the corporations—fertilizer and chemical companies, machine companies, the railroads, and the banks—who are reaping the profits.

THE COUNTRY
GRAVEYARD

A place for remembrance

It is coming up time for our annual graveyard clean-up. It is a casual event. Some Monday evening in late spring, the neighbours load spades, shovels, and lawnmowers into half-ton trucks and meet at the Mitchellton graveyard. Everyone checks out family plots first, trimming long grass and weeds and filling in gopher holes. Then a united attack is made on grass, brush, and badger holes in the rest of the area. The fence and gate are checked, perhaps a few staples replaced or a post straightened. After mower motors stop humming, news and views are exchanged at the entrance, the half-tons are reloaded, and the cemetery resumes its solitude. It is left to itself except for an occasional burial in a family plot or a visitor checking the metal plaque at the gate in search of family history.

There are similar several-acre plots all over the west. Most of them are well tended, but a few were abandoned as the local population vanished. North of us in the hills, in an abandoned cemetery, somebody once planted caragana on a loved one's grave. Caragana was about the only plant that could survive in the dusty 1930s. That caragana reproduced itself and now covers a good part of the site with an impenetrable thicket. One little heart-shaped gravestone can be seen from the road—the only sign that tells passers-by that here is a place of memories.

A few miles from Cadillac, more than ninety years ago, before a community graveyard was established, a little boy was buried beside his home. When I was a child, I remember seeing the mound and wooden cross beside a farmhouse on the south side of the highway whenever we travelled from Cadillac to Ponteix. The last time we drove on Highway 13, I noticed that the mound and cross were still there, cared for by the people who live there now.

Today we use professionals at hospitals and funeral homes. We buy perpetual care for plots marked by flat bronze plates—flat to facilitate the use of commercial mowers operated by commercial concerns. We are almost insulated from death. When I was a child, death and burial were community events. Neighbours dug the grave, the funeral was held in the local church, and friends carried the coffin into the graveyard. Using leather reins from their horses' harnesses, they gently lowered the coffin into the grave. After the family left, neighbours replaced the earth and tucked flowers onto the mound. No bright green plastic grass, no shiny hearses, no pageant to mask the reality. Only the comfort of friends doing what needed to be done.

Yet some of that tradition remains as neighbours gather to tidy graves and remember old friends. A country graveyard may not be the most lonesome place to be laid to rest, after all.

WHAT MAKES
A COMMUNITY?

A world community?
Not close enough for me

Apparently, the whole world is our community these days. With radio, television, and the Internet, our reach is wide. On news programmes and documentaries, we see young, beautiful, athletic bodies run, ski, dive, and leap, and we hear world leaders explain, complain, and spout alibis and lies. We watch floods in Bangladesh wash people and homes away like corks in a stream, tornadoes in Oklahoma wreck entire towns, earthquakes in Turkey and Japan twist metal like crumpled foil, and famine in East Africa turn men, women, and children into ragged scarecrows, scarcely able to shuffle in the dust. We can read on the faces of old men and women a history of hardship endured and hope for a brighter future for their children. Oh, the world is your neighbourhood all right, but there's a vague sense of distance about it all. What we have gained in width we have lost in depth.

A community used to be bounded by how far one could drive with horses and return home by nightfall—perhaps several school districts, thirty homes in all, sometimes with only a dozen surnames among them in rural areas. Or it could be a small town of several hundred people and farms near enough to send their children to the village school. A community was not always an Eden of harmony and goodwill, but there was a closeness, a spirit of co-operation and caring that we are losing today.

The pace of life was slower, as if geared to the quiet plodding power of horse-drawn equipment. Back home on Sunday mornings, Lutheran families gathered at a country church, while in town others went to one of the Catholic, United, Holiness Movement, or Anglican churches that were lined up along Main Street. Even the resident atheist refrained from field work on Sunday. After the church service, little groups gathered outside to exchange news and arrange ball practice, church or school clean-up bees, or maybe a picnic or berry-picking excursion.

People used to visit each other, drop in unannounced, maybe stay for supper. Nowadays we feel as if we need an excuse to visit, and we check by phone to make sure it's convenient. We are losing our neighbourliness. Farms are bigger, and farmers are fewer. Small towns are losing population and business to competition from larger centres. The detachment of a city, where folks don't know the names of the people next door, is becoming the rule, not the exception.

I suppose we can't stop progress, if that is what you call it, but we try. Mitchellton, our little town, no longer has a store, school, railroad, or church. All that's left is the community hall, where we still meet for a Christmas program and supper, an occasional 4-H whist drive, the ball tournament in June, and showers for prospective brides. Unfortunately many of the recent gatherings have been farewell parties for "used-to-be" neighbours who've retired and are moving to a place where they don't have to buck winter roads to shop or see a doctor. Their kids have scattered across the country, as have ours.

When we were kids, fifteen families lived within two miles of our home. Now we have six. And yet, last January, more than a hundred friends and relatives gathered to help us celebrate our golden wedding anniversary. True enough, a day's journey is now farther than a horse can take us, but that can be a good thing. I like to believe our own community hasn't vanished, just expanded.

Garry, Carl, and Julian Kopperud—members of the Boule Creek hardball team

Eileen Comstock

I went to school in a little white schoolhouse in Boule Creek. The community was noted for good softball teams, great Christmas concerts, and a new teacher nearly every year, because my dad, uncles, and other young farmers kept marrying them. After taking Grades Nine and Ten by correspondence, I attended Cadillac High School. Those were happy days. I especially remember the high school plays, high jinks in the chemistry lab, skating parties at the outdoor rink, and a special singing group of four or five of us who were often asked to perform at local functions.

Toward the end of World War II, I borrowed some money from my dad and took the two-month teacher-training summer course that had been set up to recruit warm bodies to fill teaching positions. My first teaching position was at Elm Springs, near Wood Mountain, with twenty-some children, including five who were taking Grades Nine or Ten by correspondence. I would like to be able to do that year over again, as I sure learned a lot about teaching at their expense. It's sort of like your first child—you should be allowed to throw it away after all the experimenting. After my second year of teaching at Welcome School north of Assiniboia, I took advantage of another summer term at Normal School (as teacher training was then called) and got a proper certificate. Mr. Fraser, my superintendent, and Mr. Andrews, the principal of the Normal School, recruited me for the job of taking Normal School students into my classroom for their practice teaching, at Mitchellton School. It was flattering to be chosen, but it was quite stressful, as there would be a visit from some inspector or other nearly every week. From there I was asked to serve as vice-principal at Limerick and then at Spring Valley.

When I taught at Mitchellton I met a young farmer, Evert Comstock. I mentioned that young farmers often found their wives-to-be teaching in the local school. Well, history repeated itself. Several years after we met, Evert and I were married on a Friday, January 14, 1949, at my home country church. It was a beautiful sunny day, and neighbours had ploughed snow for several days so that everyone could get there. The wedding was at eleven, and Mom provided dinner for the whole works in the church basement.

Our first farming years included being dried out, rusted out, and grasshoppered out, so after my first son, Lyle, was born, I taught at Bishopric, a private school, to help out. Seven years later, another child, Keith, came along, and two years after that, a daughter, Karen. In that eleven-year period Ev had a stroke from an aneurism in his head and a severe kidney infection; we bought more farmland—with a house that was bigger, warmer, and not as dilapidated as the one we first lived in; we planted more trees, remodelled buildings, and built a shop for Ev.

I kept busy mothering, 4-H-ing, helping with church and school activities, and later on started substitute teaching at Mossbank School. When the children grew up and moved out, and Ev's parents retired to Moose Jaw, I started actively helping with the farming and found it a lot more fun than housekeeping. Ev co-operated by pitching in with the house chores. By the time I hit fifty-five I decided if I were ever going to do all the fun things I wanted to, I had better start. I kind of thought that the world would stop turning when I quit the organizations and volunteer work, but it didn't. I took up ceramics, first just doing up greenware, but I soon turned to hand modelling and also started oil painting classes. I have this notion that I am capable of doing anything I really want to and probably overestimate my ability, but it is all fun, especially because I do not have to try to make a living at it.

So far I have written up a lot of our family's history, a cookbook for teens, some stories for children, and a travel book, but the only writing I have made any money out of are humorous pieces that tell about things as they were back in the good old days. Maybe that is because, though I have very little creative imagination, I do have an excellent memory.

My next birthday will be my seventy-fourth, and I am looking forward to many, many more. There have to be many more so that I can finish all the things I have started and get started on a few more things I would still like to try. Meanwhile, I still garden and keep up the yard, help with harvest and other farming stuff like bleeding brakes, fetching repairs, and holding things just so when Ev is fixing them. We now have seven grandchildren to keep track of, but unfortunately do not see them very often. Every year my siblings and our spouses have a bonding session at some resort or hotel where we eat unwisely, talk a lot, compare memories, and enjoy each other immensely.

Life is good. I've been blessed.